ANDRÉ KERTÉSZ

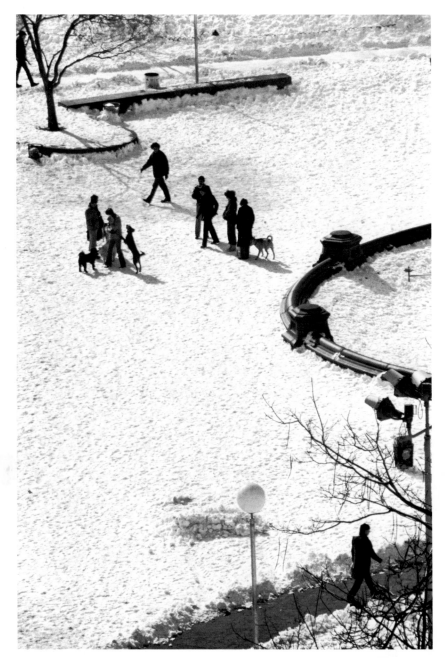

1969

ANDRÉ KERTÉSZ

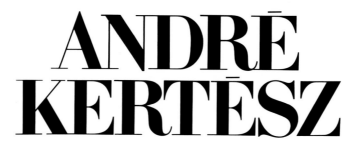

A Lifetime of Perception

Jane Corkin
Introduction by Ben Lifson

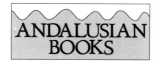

ANDALUSIAN
BOOKS

ISBN 0-9637867-0-9

Andalusian Books
1133 Broadway, Suite #1429
New York, N.Y. 10010

Designed by Ken Rodmell
Printed and bound in Spain

*André Kertész was a man whose allegiance to personal
values and ideals crossed all boundaries and spoke to all people.
Through this work he exposed his heart and soul and left us with
a record of human experience. To be associated with a man of
Mr. Kertész' principle and integrity left a profound influence
on my life. I am grateful for the time we shared.*

Jane Corkin

INTRODUCTION

In the fall of 1936, André Kertész was visited in his Montparnasse apartment by a French government official. France, said the visitor, wished to acknowledge the 42-year-old Hungarian photographer's artistic contribution to the country he had lived in since 1925; would he accept honorary citizenship? But Kertész was about to leave for New York and a year's work with an American photo agency. Touched, he promised to notify the government immediately on his return to Paris when he would accept the award.

In New York, Kertész was first neglected then exploited by his employers. When he broke his contract with them in order to freelance, editors and art directors rejected his pictures as too eloquent or too modern. By then Europe was on the verge of war; Kertész stayed in New York and continued working on the fringe of the profession he had helped to create. When the United States entered the war, and Kertész had to register as an enemy alien, he was officially advised against photographing in the streets and thus effectively barred from a major subject of his art. Moreover, curators and art dealers had difficulty reconciling his art to their ideas of signature style. Kertész struggled throughout the war, gradually fading from public view. In 1947, he abandoned photojournalism and joined the staff of Condé Nast Publications; for 14 years thereafter he produced competent, undistinguished interiors for *House and Garden*. He became an American citizen in 1944, and thereafter returned to Europe only as a visitor.

From the beginning of his life in the United States, in spite of the American art world's neglect, Kertész kept working in the style that had established him as one of Europe's leading photographic artists. This effort gradually assumed heroic proportions. In effect, Kertész was creating a second artistic life. Recognition did eventually return, in the form of exhibitions, grants, publications and honors, especially after he left Condé Nast in 1964 and devoted himself entirely to his art.

This book is the first to give equal weight to both Kertész' European and American careers. It portrays Kertész' continuously evolving sense of the possibilities of his art and his sense of himself from youth to old age.

Kertész bought his first camera in Budapest in 1912, at the age of 18. It was a small, primitive, hand-held instrument, and with it he began a photography based on direct observation of everyday life. Its inspiration was conventional: genre scenes (woodcuts and lithographs) in popular illustrated family magazines. But in practice it was revolutionary. At the time, large-plate pictures in imitation of painting identified the serious photographer; with his little camera, Kertész explored an idiom of pure photographic description. His creative exhilaration and his respect for life absorbed Kertész more than thoughts about his esthetic isolation.

This vision changed as Kertész fought in World War I and then after the war, as he worked at the Budapest stock exchange and endured the frustrations of the obscure artist mired in a mundane job. Dispossessed characters—gypsies, beggars, soldiers saying their farewells—appeared in his work and fit uneasily into its frames. Kertész also began to experiment with tense picture structures, distortions and prints turned upside down; he was discovering for himself what modernist artists everywhere were then consolidating; the independence of the work of art from the world it described. Still, his work sustained its illusion of literalism, and his maturing wit and growing sense of alienation contended with his view of the world as sweet, mysterious and beautiful. This unprecedented photography distanced Kertész still further from traditional photographic circles but drew him to Budapest's avant-garde.

To Hungarian artists, a sojourn in a European art capital was an obligatory rite of passage. But to Kertész, his departure for Paris was a search for a new artistic home. Artists as disparate as Mondrian and the Surrealists recognized aspects of their own concerns in his work; soon he was exhibiting and publishing in avant-garde circles. European photojournalism was then in its infancy, and Kertész rapidly became one of its most widely published pioneers and a leading stylist.

Kertész absorbed much from his new milieu. Allusions to flatness, abstraction and collage began to appear in his work. In his disorienting views of Paris from above and in his distorted nudes of 1933, his original tension between surface pattern and deep space became specifically modernist. The life of the capital—its styles, movement and modernity—replaced Kertész' earlier concern for provincial life. Portraits of Mondrian, Chagall, Calder, Eisenstein and others appeared as Kertész took his place among Paris' emigré artists. Yet he maintained his connection with common life, and although his *bals musettes*, music halls and street fairs reflected Surrealist taste in popular art, his tramps and wounded war veterans sprang from his own understanding of homelessness. Still, in the emigré city he created, charm and companionship prevail.

Kertész' access to the grace and surprise that punctuate the everyday flow of life in the streets, was facilitated by the newly invented Leica camera, which he was the first serious photographer to master. Its ease and speed permitted unobtrusive observation of intimate moments

and several variations on an initial pictorial idea within seconds; with it Kertész sensed boundless possibility. In *Meudon, 1929*, a man holding what looks like a painting wrapped in a newspaper crosses a busy suburban street; at the end of the street, a train steams across a viaduct that evokes both ancient Rome and the world of de Chirico. With photographs like this, Kertész embraced modernism's fascination with chance and disjunction. His Parisian photography flowed back and forth across the stylistic boundaries of the genre scene, documentary literalism and abstraction; at his best he created a stylistic amalgam similar in spirit to late Cubism's blend of different styles of draftsmanship within a single canvas. He had established himself as a shaper of the art of a modernist capital.

In the Paris work, the photographer's persona is also free: not quite earthbound, somewhat detached from history, he governs time, observes style and creates as much as describes his urban space. This is an idealized persona whose home is art. But in New York, history and chance converted voluntary emigration into exile. Because Kertész couldn't adapt his work to American expectations, his stylistic pluralism worked against him. Art now became a refuge.

He kept photographing from above, for example, as he had in Paris, but the city he created was remote and blank, its citizens stilled, waiting and dwarfed. As Kertész withdrew from public life, his style shed its earlier descriptive and spatial amplitude and became terse, planar, angular and abstract; its surprises stemmed less from the city's flux than the photographer's arbitrariness. His wit grew mordant and grotesque as disembodied arms and headless figures—often blatantly the function of Kertész' framing—haunted streets which were, themselves, abruptly isolated from their larger contexts. This work is ironically distant from its subjects, its pictorial beauty an assertion of the artist's power. It is a private matter.

After leaving Condé Nast in 1962, and with the gradual return of recognition, Kertész' work took on a renewed complexity and delicacy, especially in his scenes of Washington Square Park from above. But even here the human figures, although at ease in the park's lush intricacy, hardly notice its beauty, which we perceive as a thing of the artist's fashioning. Kertész' high vantage point suggests his own emotional distance and a concern for artifice. Only on Kertész' several trips abroad after 1964 did his earlier humor reappear in pictures which also looked more seen than made. But here, as in most of the work since 1936, there was no real return to the imagery of public buildings, monuments and cafés which once located Kertész' work and spirit within the larger public world.

For the last 32 years of his life, Kertész lived in an apartment high above Washington Square Park in Greenwich Village. Despite occasional problems with dizziness and tremors in his hands that he experienced in the last decade of his life, he continued to photograph constantly, turning the constraints of age into the terms of new creativity.

From the balcony of his apartment, Kertész pointed his camera down on MacDougal Alley, where branches tangled with their shadows on the snow. Although his Parisian buoyancy had changed to vertigo and the nights were colder than when he learned to photograph them in Budapest in 1917, he photographed with the effortlessness and economy of a virtuoso, turning the limited subject matter at his disposal into compelling imagery that recalls the wit and charm of his early work. Kertész orchestrated figures in the park into scenes that have the delicacy of lace and that evoke Breughel — or Kertész. Although the figures in these later photographs are no smaller or more remote than those in his Paris and Budapest images, they are frequently mere silhouettes, and exist one degree further from life than their earlier counterparts.

In New York at the beginning, as in Budapest at the beginning, Kertész worked alone. But in Budapest recognition came by the early 1920s; in New York Kertész had to wait 28 years for his first one-man exhibition at the Museum of Modern Art. Confirmation of his continuing worth had to come from within, from the work itself, and because the art world effectively ignored him and he withdrew from it, his standard gradually became his own earlier work. When honors came, they too referred mainly to his European career. During the last 15 years of his life, he spent much of his time editing and publishing his old work.

But he also continued to photograph. Confident that his art had rejoined the world, he photographed the world as if it were a continuing set of variations on his own pictures.

Using many of the beautiful objects he collected over the years, Kertész constructed coincidence on his desk and windowsills. He photographed with so light a touch that the scenes of Botticelli's Venus done in glass, a Last Supper in stone and more mundane objects, look observed, not arranged. They evoke the earlier street pictures and their poetry of chance. They also refer us to the still-life Kertész made in Mondrian's house and Leger's studio more than 50 years earlier. But in these works, the eyeglasses, knick-knacks and original art works were Kertész'. Their settings — windowsills, desks littered with correspondence, shelves full of art books, including Kertész' — describe the boundaries of this late work: the extreme privacy of the apartment, the past, Kertész' newly won public milieu, and mortality.

As the world and his work merged, the world Kertész described represents his innermost thoughts and emotions. The still-lifes are homages to love, outbursts of anger, farewells to the flesh and intimations of mortality.

Kertész photographed birds throughout his career. They alluded to the creative spirit and Kertész' sense of confinement and neglect. Whether flying with their shadows or made of glass and perched on his windowsill, they became metaphors for a photographer who hovered between life and the expectation of death, who saw himself as already part of artistic history, yet still involved in creating new work.

From the beginning, Kertész' photography was praised for describing common sights as if the photographer were seeing them for the first time with a child-like wonder and an unembarrassed expression of sentiment. Turning to symbolism later in life, he found it possible to look at approaching death, artistic fame and the transformation of active love into active memory, with the candor, playfulness and curiosity of his earliest pictures, which persuaded us he was looking only at the world.

Ben Lifson, New York

CHRONOLOGY

1894
Born July 2 in Budapest, Hungary.

1912
Received baccalaureate from the Academy of Commerce, Budapest.
Employed as a clerk in the Budapest Stock Exchange.
Bought his first camera, an ICA box camera (with 4.5 × 6 cm plates).

1913
Bought an ICA Bebe (with 4.5 × 6 cm plates) and a Voigtländer Alpine (with 9 × 12 cm plates).

1914-1918
Served in the Austro-Hungarian Army. Wounded in 1915. Photographed behind the lines and during the Commune with a Goerz Tenax (with 4.5 × 6 cm plates). Most of Kertész' negatives were destroyed during the Hungarian Revolution.

1916
Received "last prize" from *Borsszem Janko* magazine for a satiric self-portrait entered in a competition of war photography.

1917
Published first photographs in *Erdekes Ujsag* (an early picture magazine, a precursor of *Life*.) First cover photograph in 1925.

1918
Resumed employment with the Budapest Stock Exchange.

1923
Offered a silver medal by the Hungarian Amateur Photographers' Association, but only on the condition he print the picture in bromoil in the style of salon photography. Turned the medal down and accepted diploma instead.

1925
Moved to Paris.

1925-1928
Did free-lance reportage for the following publications:

France—*Le Sourire, Variétés, Le Matin, L'Intransigeant, Art vivant*; Germany—*Uhu, Frankfurter Illustrierte, Berliner Illustrierte Zeitung, Strasburger Illustrierte, Münchener Illustrierte Presse, Kölnische Illustrierte Zeitung, Illustrierte Zeitung Leipzig, Die Dame, Das Illustrierte Blatt, Neue Jugend, Das Tageblatt, Die Photographie*; Italy—*La Nazione Firenze*; Great Britain—*The Times, The Sketch, The Sphere*.

1927
First one-man exhibition at Sacre du Printemps Gallery.

1928
Bought first Leica camera.
Exhibited in the "First Independent Salon of Photography" at the Théâtre des Champs Élysées.
Vu magazine began publication. Kertész was a major contributor (until 1936).
Worked with Ribémont-Dessaignes on the revue *Bifur* (until 1930).

1929
Sold photographs to the collections of the Staätliche Museen Kunstbibliothek in Berlin and the König-Albert Museum in Zwickau.
Exhibited in "Contemporary Photography" at Essen.
Exhibited 30 photographs in "Film und Foto" at Stuttgart.

1930
Received a silver medal at the Exposition Coloniale, Paris.
Exhibited photographs in Munich.
Art et Médecine began publication. Kertész became a major contributor (until 1936).

1932
Exhibited 35 photographs in "Modern European Photography" at the Julien Levy Gallery, New York.
Exhibited photographs in Brussells.

1933
Married Elizabeth Sali of Budapest.
First book, *Enfants*, was published. Text by Jaboune. Paris: Éditions d'Histoire et d'Art. 54 photographs.

1934
Exhibited ten photographs with ten other photographers

at Leleu's in Paris (Leleu was a well-known interior decorator). Exhibited in "Groupe annuel des photographies" at Galerie de la Pléiade, Paris.
Paris Vu Par André Kertész is published. Text by Pierre Mac-Orlan. Paris: Éditions d'Histoire et d'Art. 48 photographs.

1936
Nos Amies les Bêtes is published. Text by Jaboune.
Paris: Éditions d'Histoire et d'Art. 60 photographs.
Moved to New York. Began a one-year contract with Keystone Studios, a major picture agency of the 1930s, under the direction of fellow Hungarian, Ernie Prince. Lived at the Beaux Arts Hotel.

1937
Exhibited five photographs in "Photography 1839-1937" curated by Beaumont Newhall at the Museum of Modern Art.
Exhibited in "Pioneers of Modern French Photography" at the Julien Levy Gallery, New York.
Les Cathédrales du Vin was published. Text by Pierre Hamp. Paris: Établissements Sainrapt et Brice. 28 photographs.
Photographs published in *Look* but credited to Ernie Prince.

1937-1949
Free-lanced for *American Magazine, Collier's, Coronet, Harper's Bazaar, House and Garden, Look, Town and Country*, and *Vogue*.

1939
Became an enemy alien. Restricted by law from photographing outdoors.

1944
Became an American citizen.

1945
Day of Paris was published. Edited by George Davis.
New York: J.J. Augustin. 126 photographs.

1946
One-man exhibition at The Art Institute of Chicago.

1949
Joined Condé Nast Publications under exclusive contract.

1962
Terminated contract with Condé Nast Publications.
One-man exhibition at Long Island University, New York.
Catalogue published: *Kertész at Long Island University*.
Text by Nathan Resnick.

1963
Retrospective exhibition, IV Mostra Biennale Internazionale della Fotografia, Venice. Awarded the gold medal.
Catalogue published.
One-man exhibition at the Bibliothèque Nationale, Paris.
Catalogue published: *André Kertész—photographies*.
Introduction by Alix Gambier.
One-man exhibition at ModernAge Studio, New York.

1964
One-man exhibition, Museum of Modern Art, New York.
André Kertész, Photographer was published. Text by John Szarkowski. New York: Museum of Modern Art.
64 photographs.

1965
Appointed honorary member of the American Society of Magazine Photographers. Guest of honor at the Miami Conference on Communication Arts, University of Miami, Coral Gables, Florida.

1966
André Kertész was published. Edited with a text by Anna Farova. Cornell Capa and Robert Sagalyn, associate editors. New York: Grossman Publishers. Paragraphic Books.
76 photographs.

1967
Exhibited in "The Concerned Photographer" at the Riverside Museum, New York. Catalogue published. New York: Grossman Publishers.

1968
"The Concerned Photographer" was shown in Matsuya, Tokyo.

1970
Exhibited ten photographs at the U.S. Pavilion, The World's Fair Expo, Tokyo.

1971
One-man exhibition at the Moderna Museet, Stockholm.
One-man exhibition at the Magyar Nemzeti Galeria, Budapest.
Catalogue published.
On Reading was published. New York: Grossman Publishers.
64 pp.

1972
One-man exhibition at The Photographers' Gallery, London.
One-man exhibition at Valokuvamuseon, Helsinki.
André Kertész: Sixty Years of Photography, 1912-1972 was published. Edited by Nicolas Ducrot. New York: Grossman Publishers. 250 photographs.

1973
One-man exhibition at the Hallmark Gallery, New York.
One-man exhibition at Light Gallery, New York.

1974
Received Guggenheim Fellowship.
J'aime Paris: Photographs Since the Twenties was
published. Edited by Nicolas Ducrot. New York:
Grossman Publishers. 219 photographs.

1975
Guest of Honor at Arles. Exhibition of photographs.
Washington Square was published. Introduction by Brendan
Gill. New York: Grossman Publishers.
104 photographs.

1976
Appointed Commander of the Order of Arts and Letters by the
French government.
One-man exhibition at Wesleyan University, Middletown,
Connecticut.
One-man exhibition at French Cultural Services, New York.
Distortions was published. Introduction by Hilton Kramer.
New York: Alfred A. Knopf. 200 photographs.
Of New York was published. New York: Alfred A. Knopf. 184
photographs.

1977
Received Mayor's Award of Honor for Arts and Culture,
New York.
Elizabeth died on October 21.
Retrospective exhibition at the Musée d'Art Modern, Centre
Beaubourg, Paris. Circulated throughout France. Catalogue
published: *André Kertész.* Edited by Contrejour. Paris:
Centre National d'Art et de Culture Georges-Pompidou.
72 photographs.
Exhibited in "Sympathetic Explorations: Kertész/Harbutt,"
Plains Art Museum, Moorhead, Minnesota. Catalogue
published. 24 plates by Kertész.
Exhibited in "Documenta 6," Kassel, West Germany.
André Kertész was published. Text by Carol Kismaric. Miller-
ton, N.Y.: Aperture Inc., The History of Photography Series.
44 photographs.

1978
Exhibited in "Neue Sachlichkeit and German Realism of the
20's," Hayward Gallery, London.

1979
One-man exhibition at the Serpentine Gallery, London..Cata-
logue published: *André Kertész.* Text by Collin Ford. London:

The Arts Council of Great Britain.
Exhibited in "La Photographie Française 1925-1940," Galerie
Zabriskie, Paris and New York.
America, *Birds*, *Landscapes*, and *Portraits* were published.
Edited by Nicolas Ducrot. New York: Mayflower Books Inc.
Each with 64 photographs.

1980
Received Medal of the City of Paris.
Received First Annual Award of the Association of
International Photography Art Dealers, New York.
Retrospective exhibition at Salford University,
Salford, England. Received a certificate of merit
from Prince Philip.
Retrospective exhibition at the Jerusalem Art Museum.
André Kertész was published. By Agathe Gaillard. Paris: Pierre
Belfond. 16 photographs.

1981
Received Mayor's Award of Honor for Arts and Culture,
New York City.
Received Honorary Doctorate of Fine Arts from Bard College,
Annandale-on-Hudson, New York.
Retrospective exhibition at Cornell Fine Arts Center, Rollins
College, Winter Park, Florida.
From My Window was published. Introduction by Peter
MacGill. Boston: New York Graphic Society. 53 SX70
color photographs.

1982
Retrospective exhibition at the Canadian Centre for
Photography, Toronto.

1983
One-man exhibition at the New York Public Library,
New York.
One-man exhibition at the Portland Art Museum, Oregon.
Appointed Officer, Légion d'Honneur by the French govern-
ment.

1984
One-man exhibition at the University of Miami, Coral Gables,
Florida.
Retrospective exhibition at the Akron Art Museum, Ohio.

1985
Retrospective exhibition at the Art Institute of Chicago,
Chicago, Illinois; exhibition travelled to the Metropolitan
Museum of Art, New York.
Died September 27 in New York.

Penelope A. Dixon

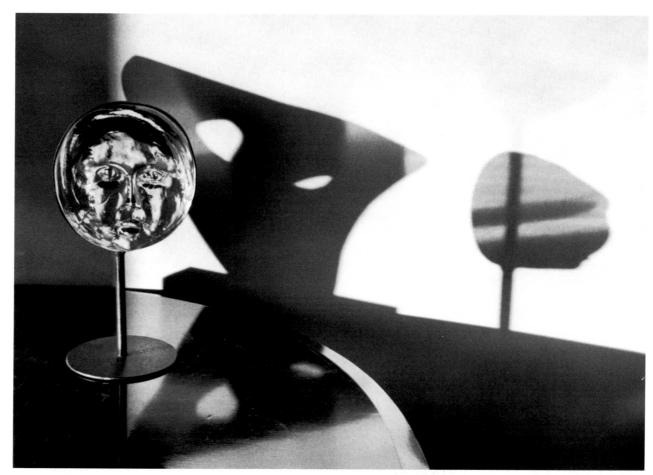

1975

PLATES

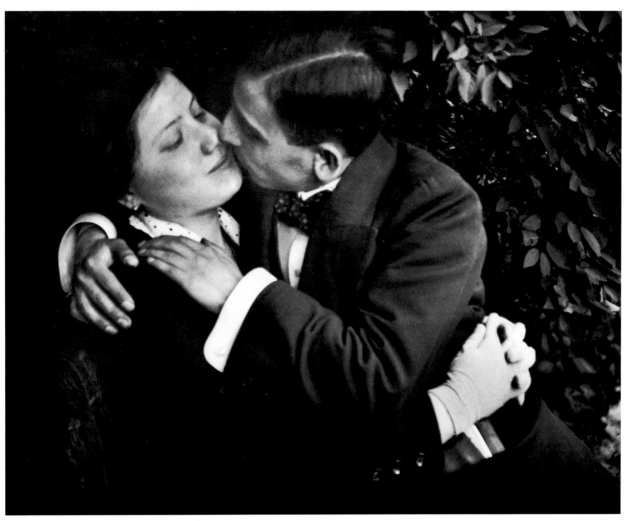

1915

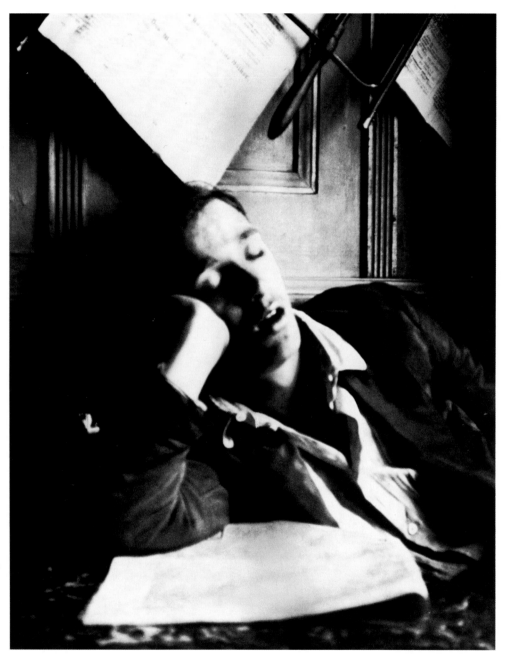

1912

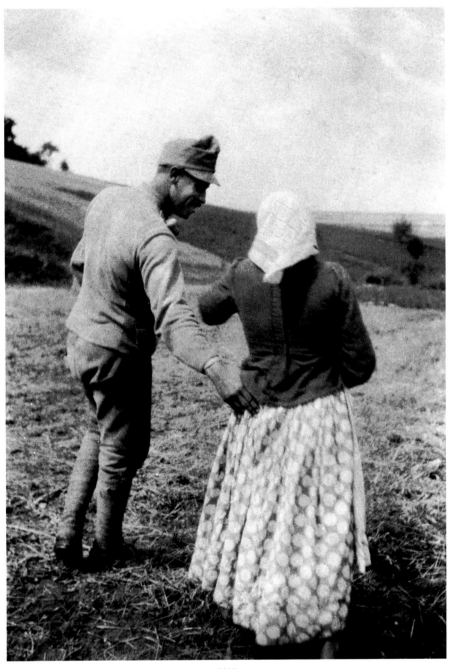

1915

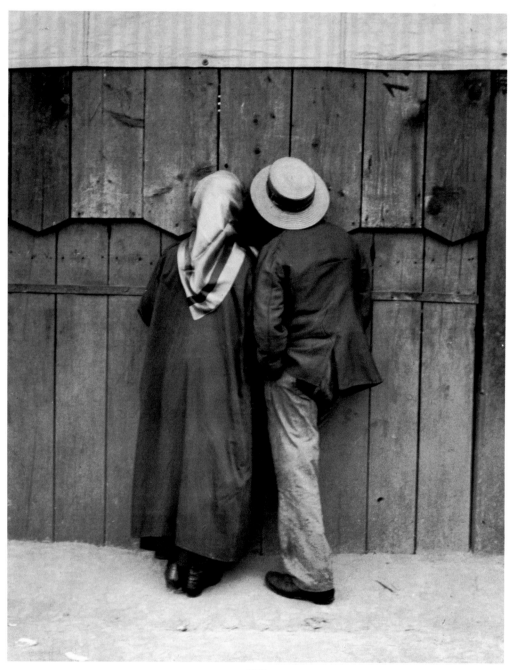

1920

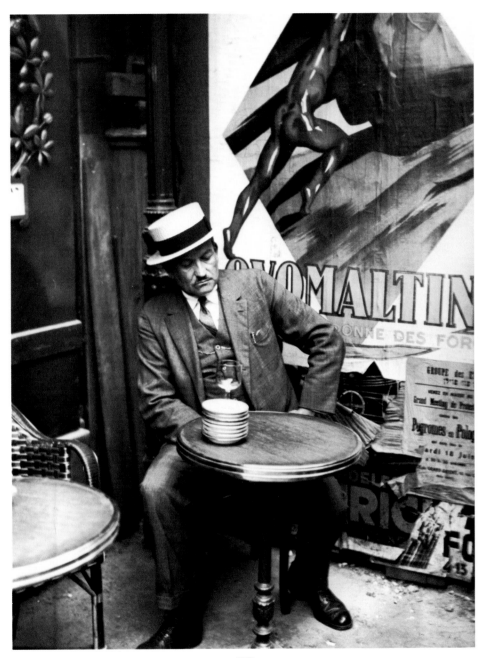

1928

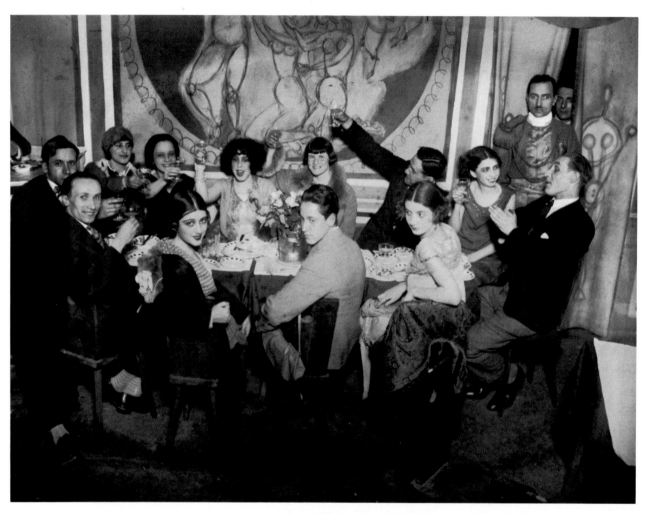

1928

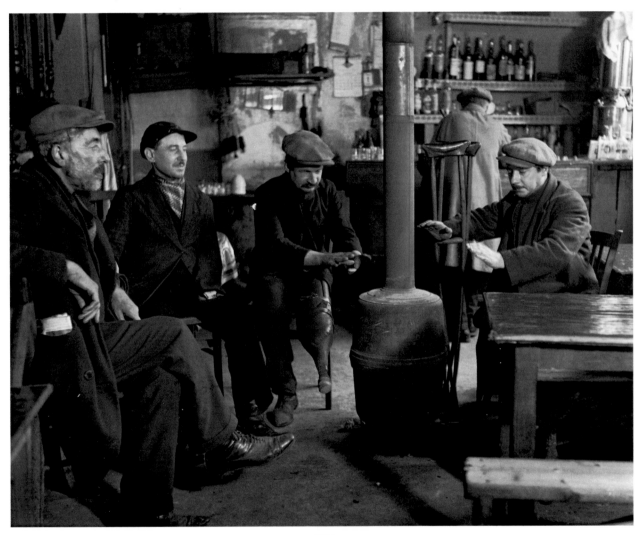

1927

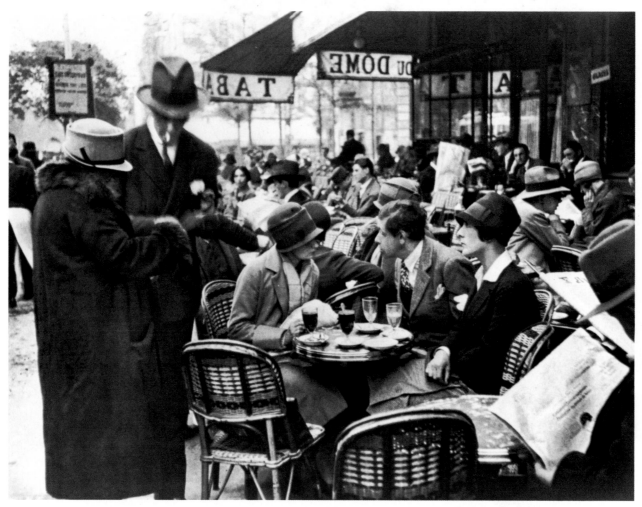

1925

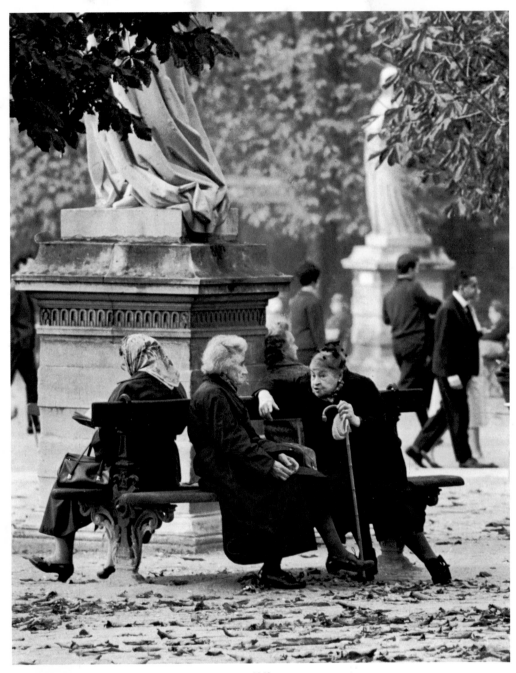

1963

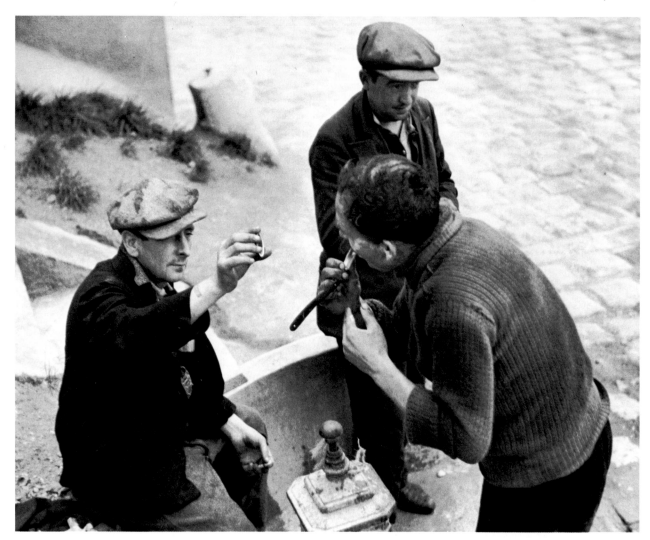

1930

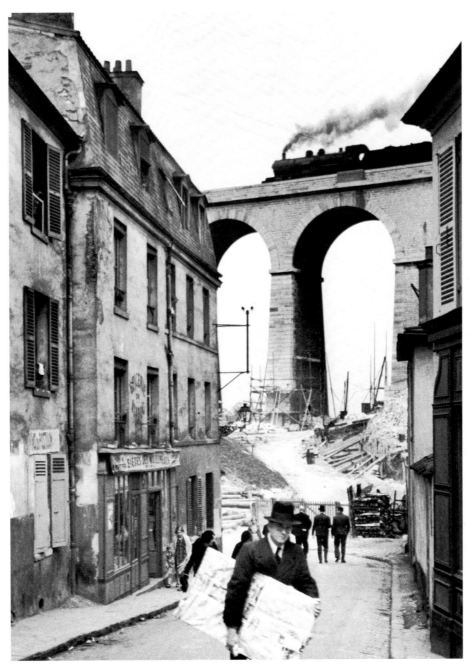

1928

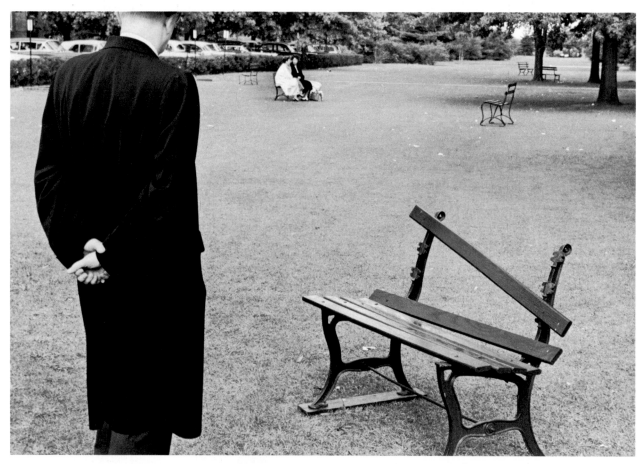

1962

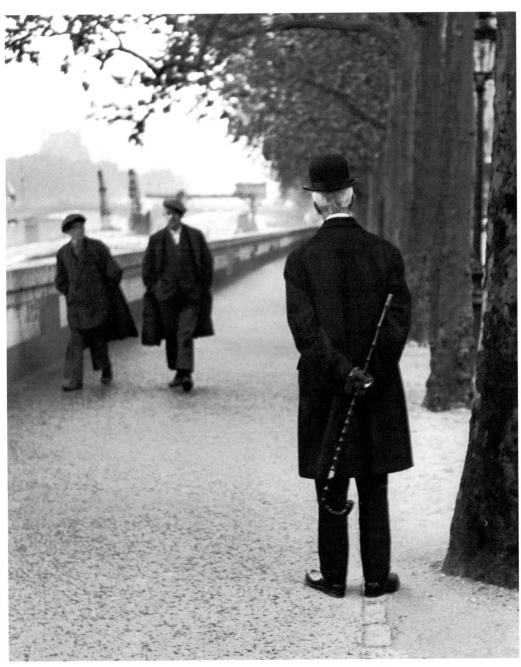

1926

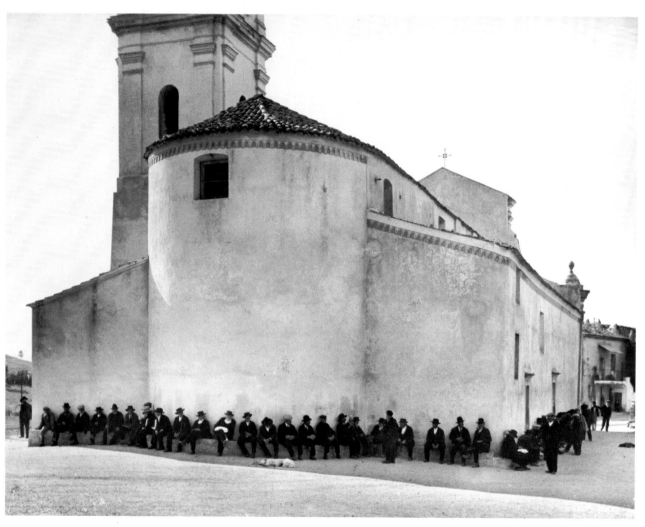

1932

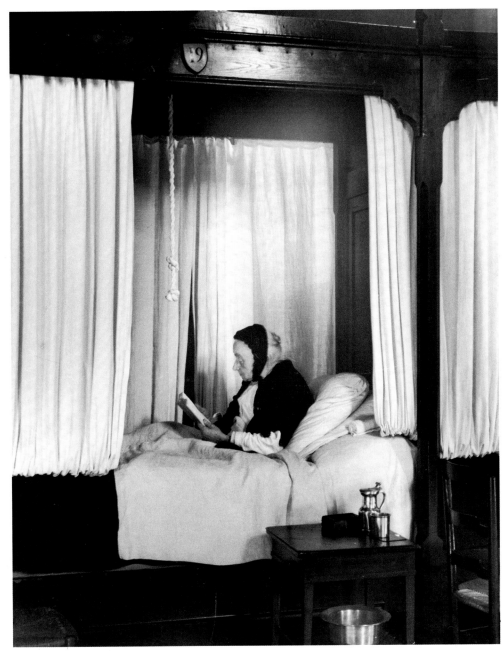

1929

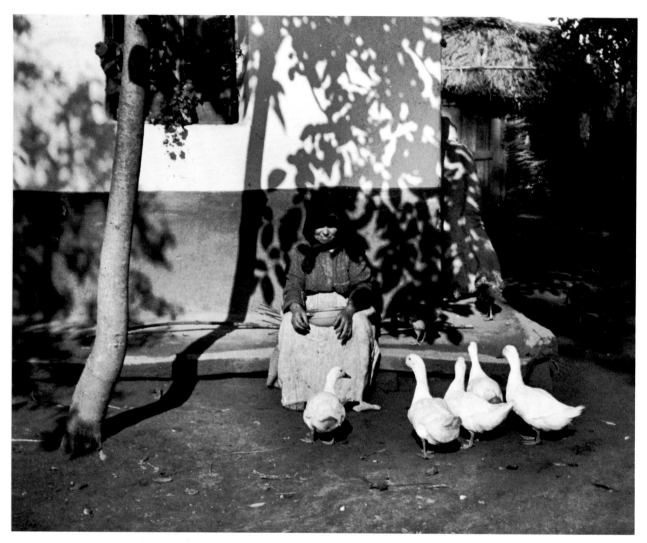

1924

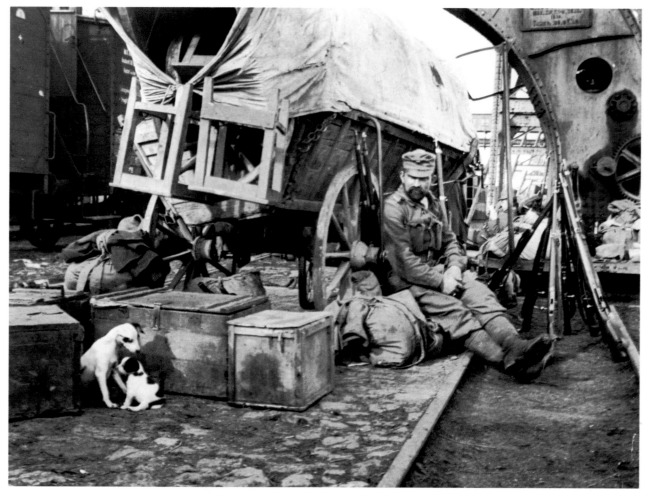

1918

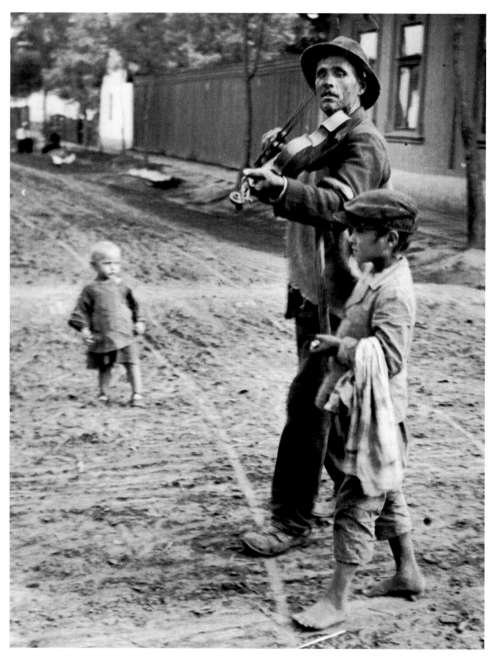

1921

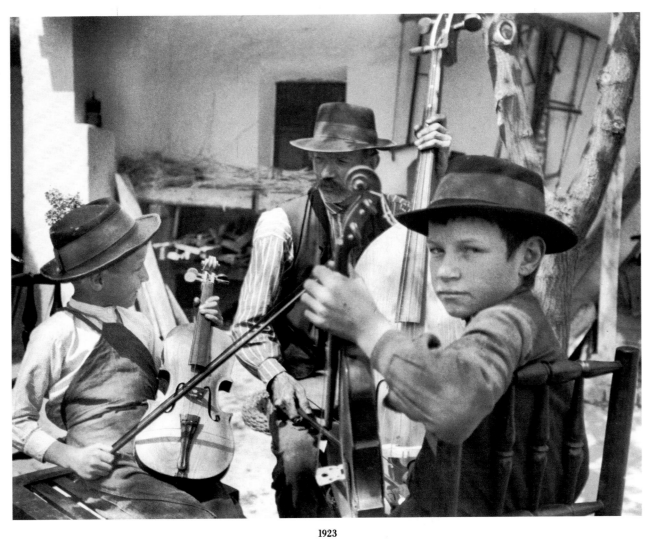

1923

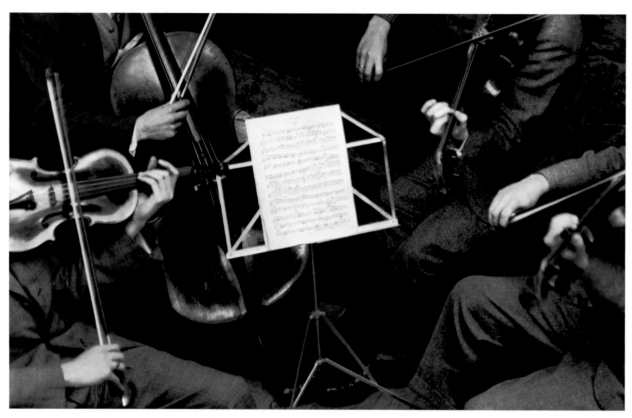

1926

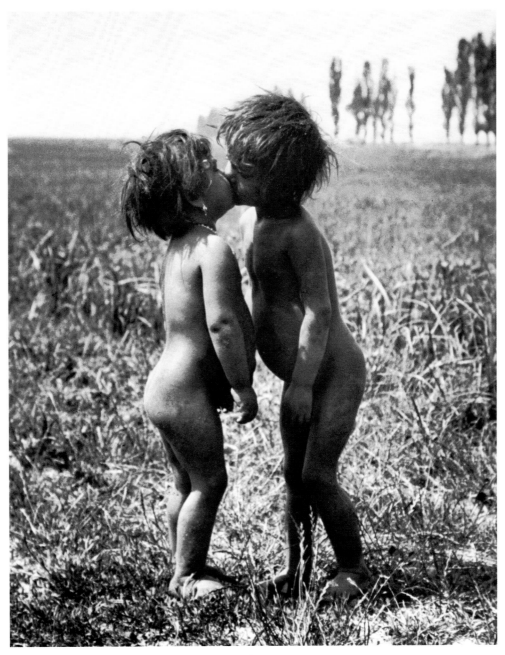

1917

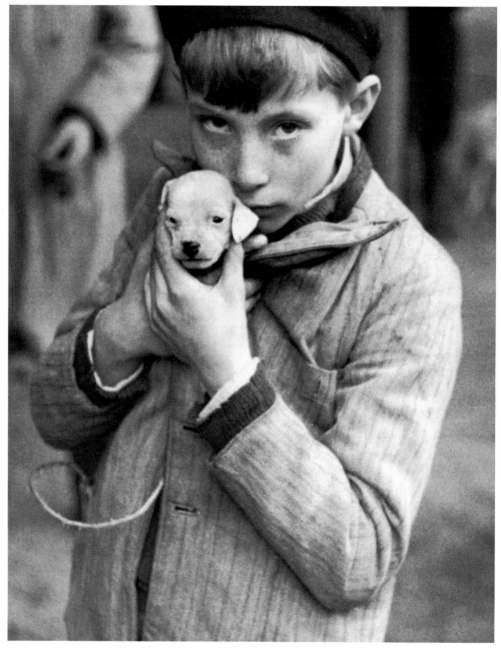

1928

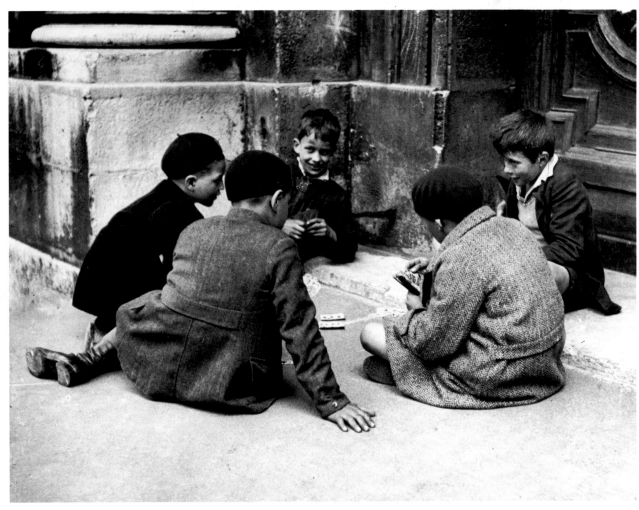

1926

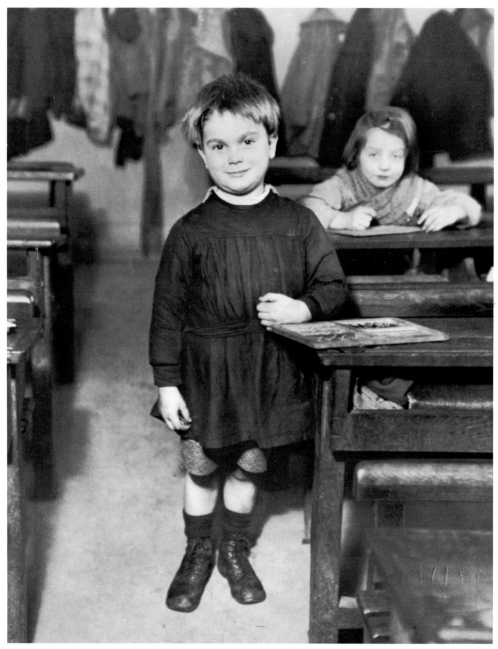

1931

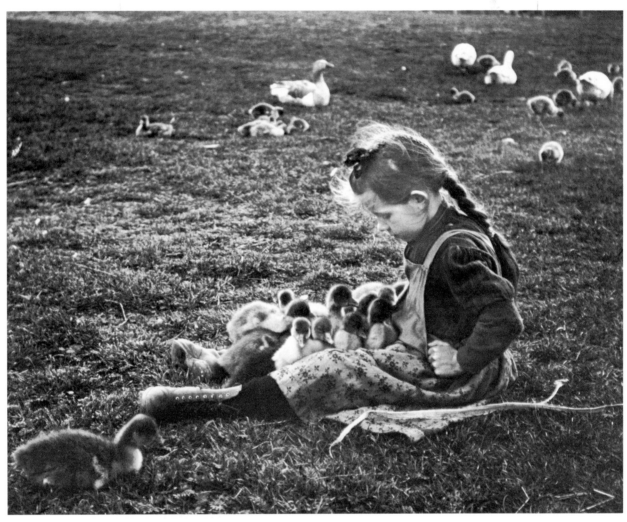

1918

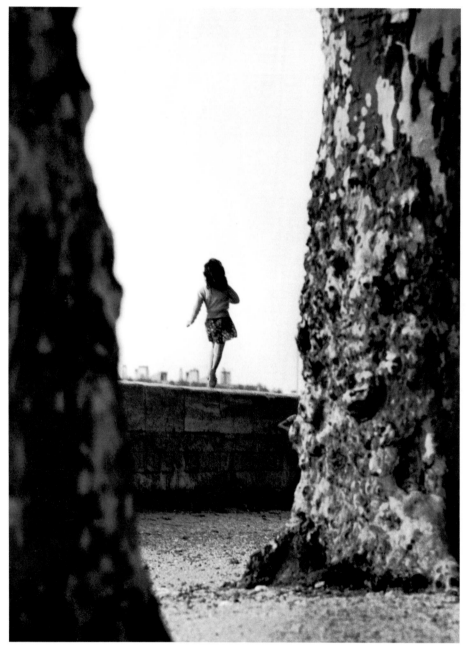

1979

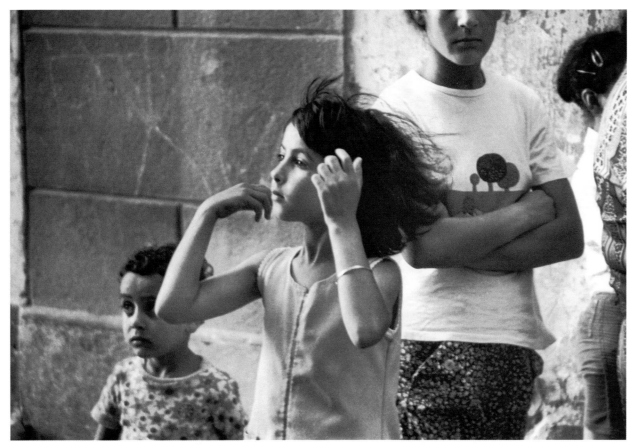

1979

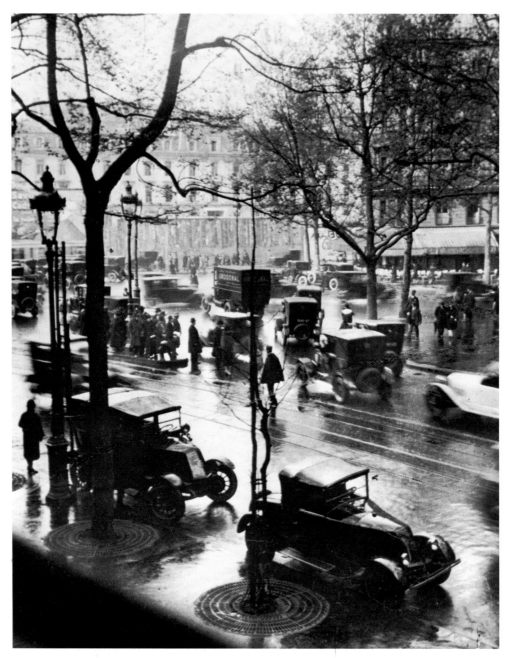

1925

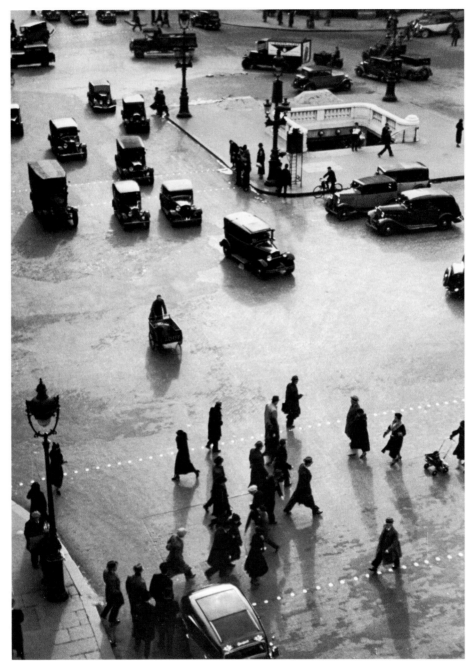

1929

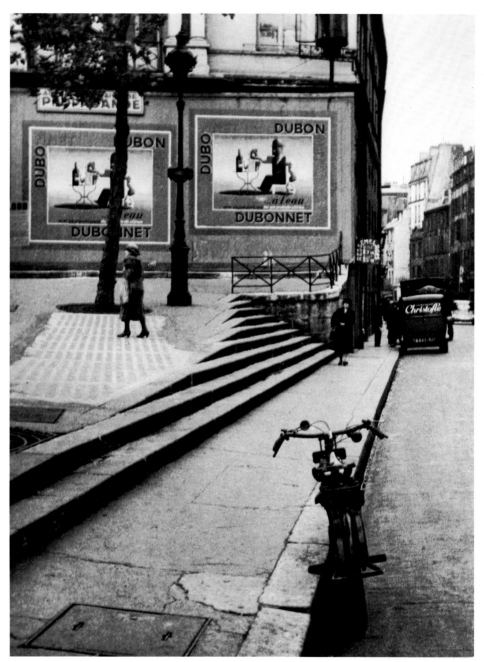

1934

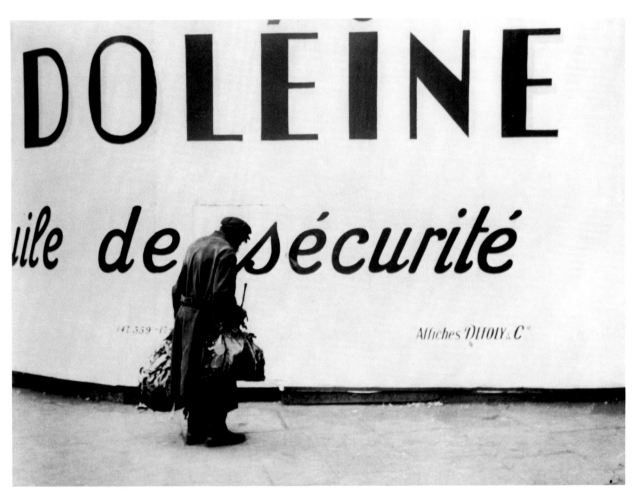

1927

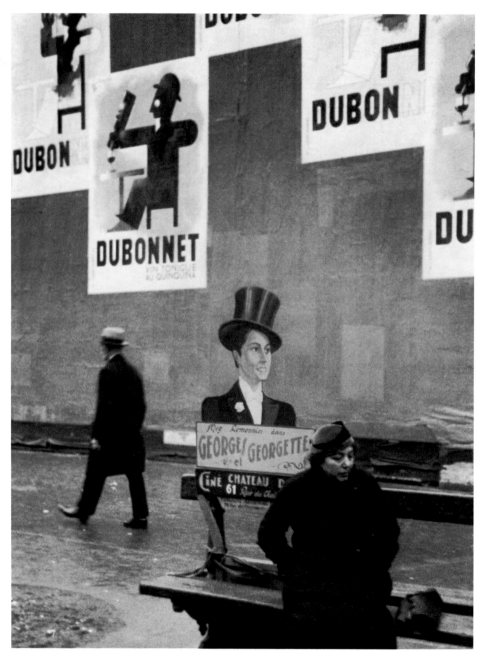

1934

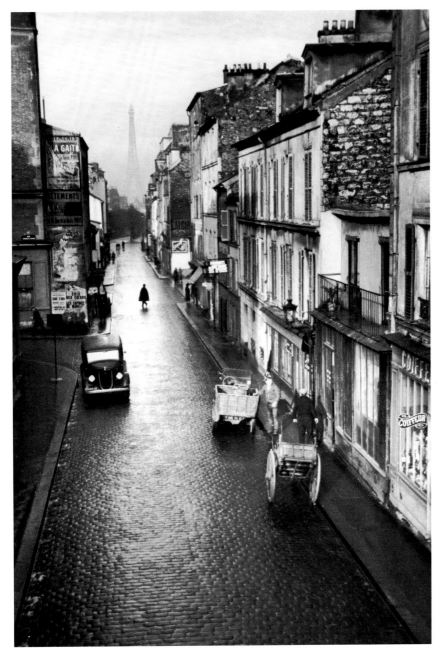

1932

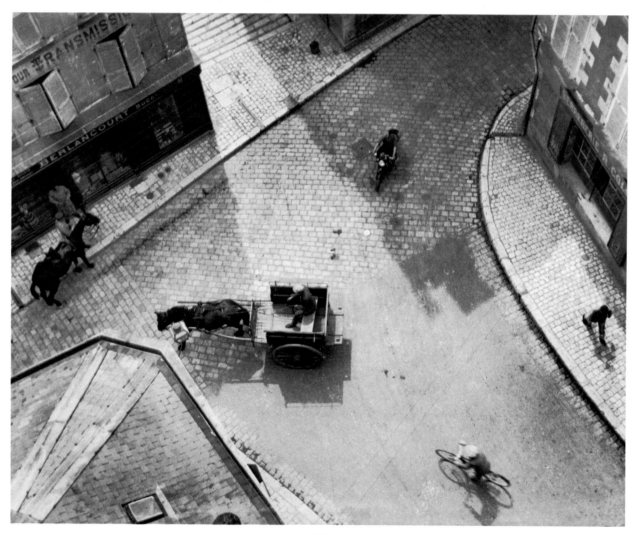

1930

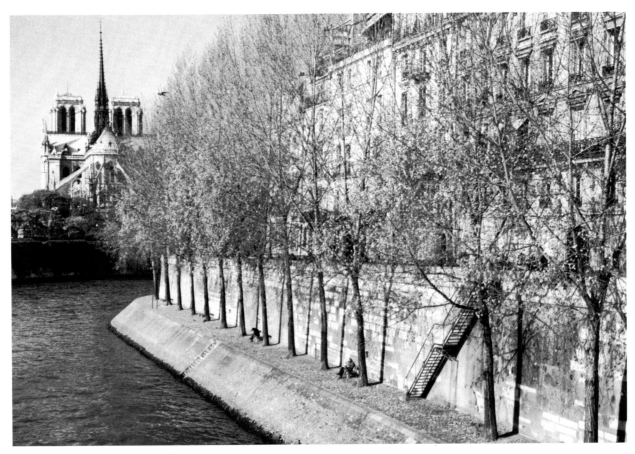

1980

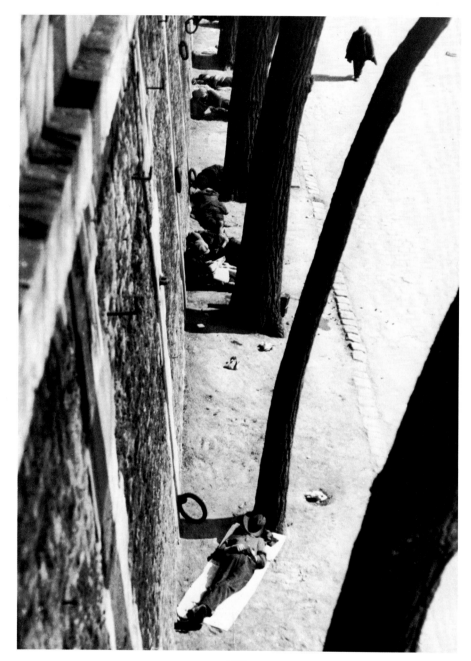

1927

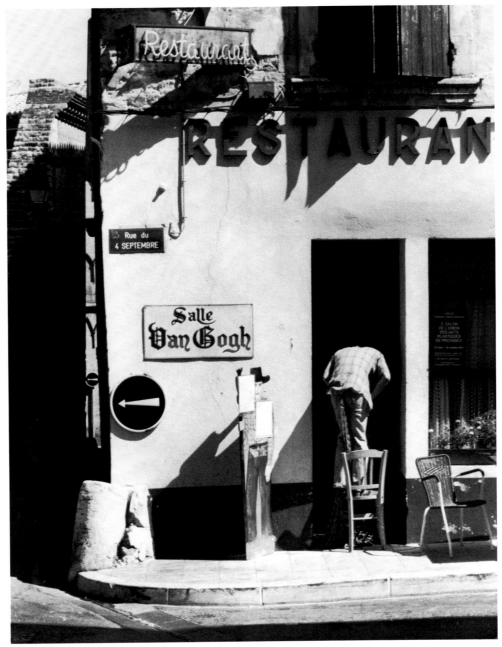

1979

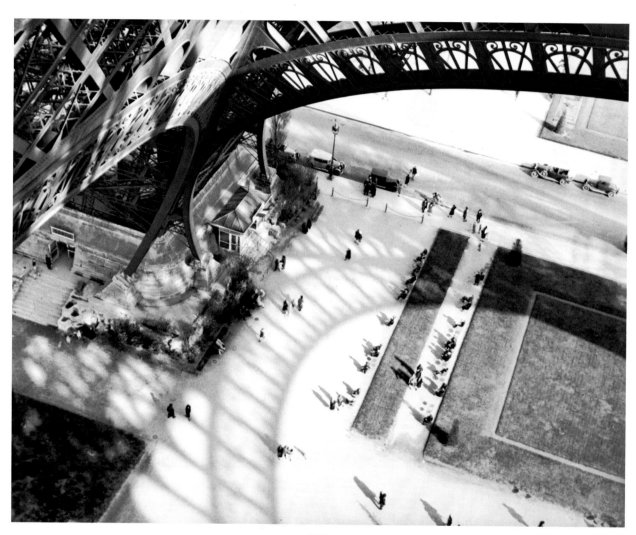

1929

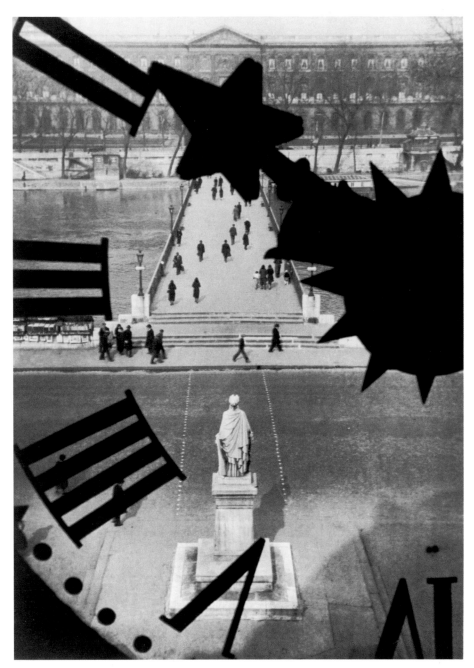

1932

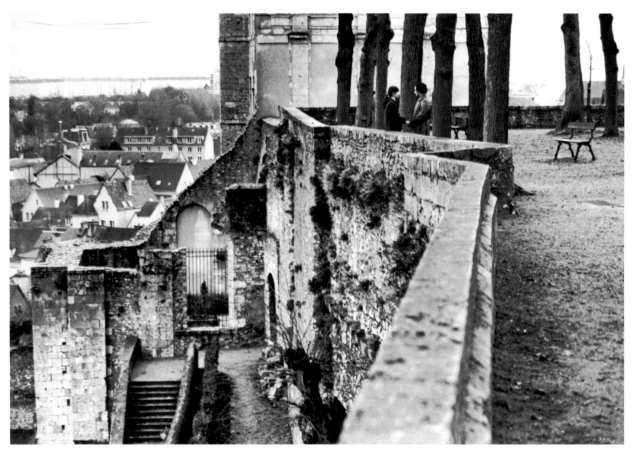

1977

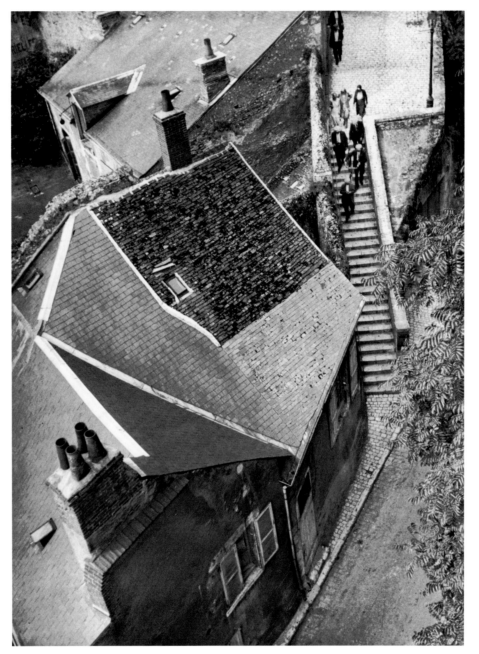

1930

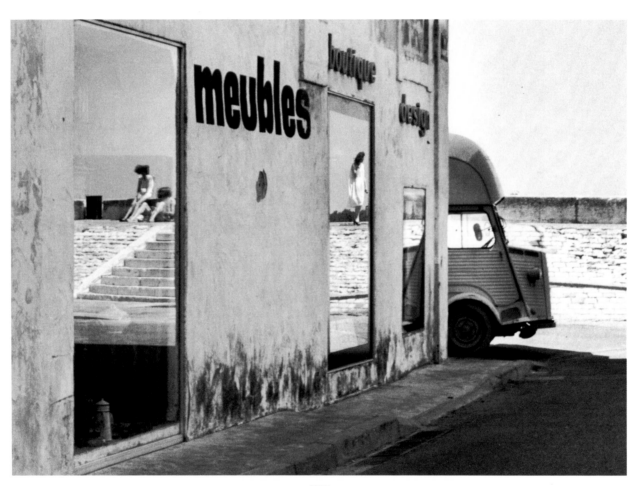

1979

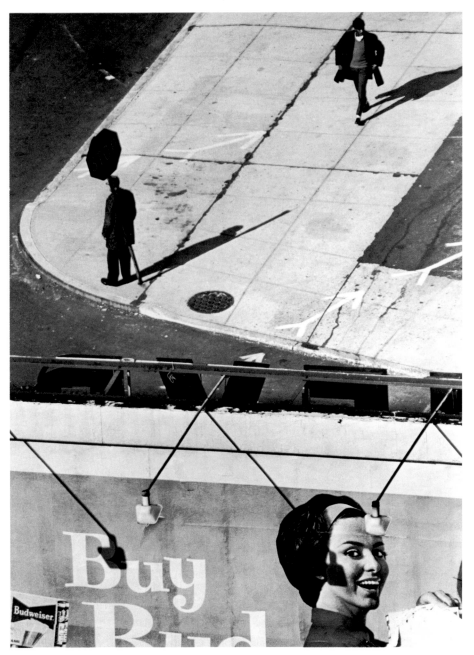

1962

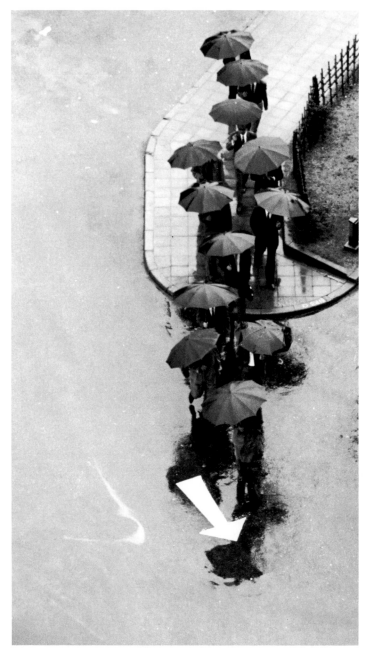

1968

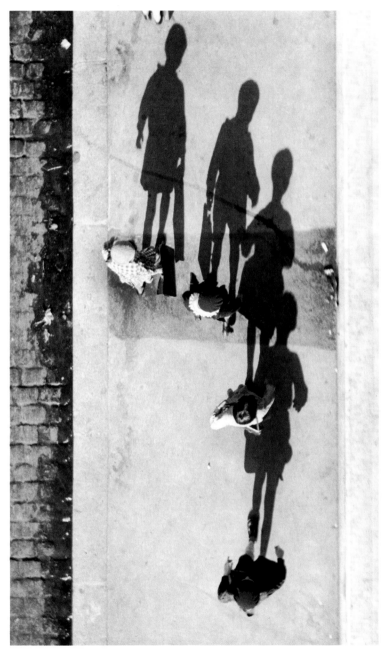

1931

57

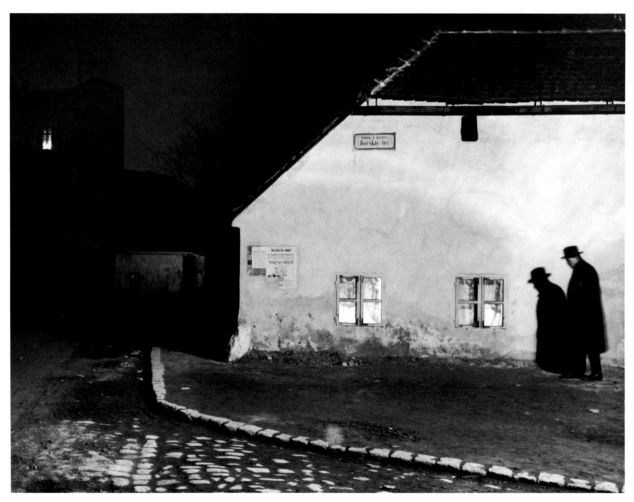

1914

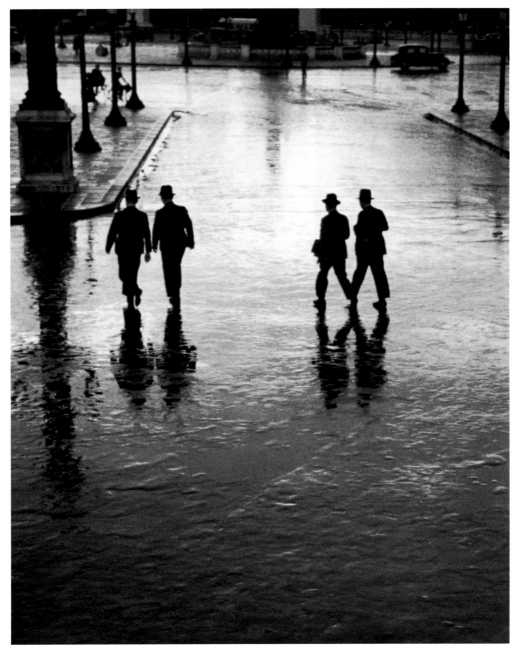

1928

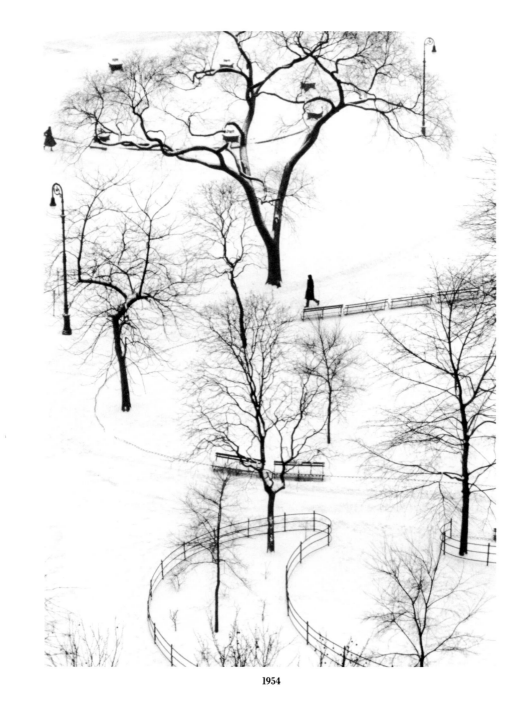

1954

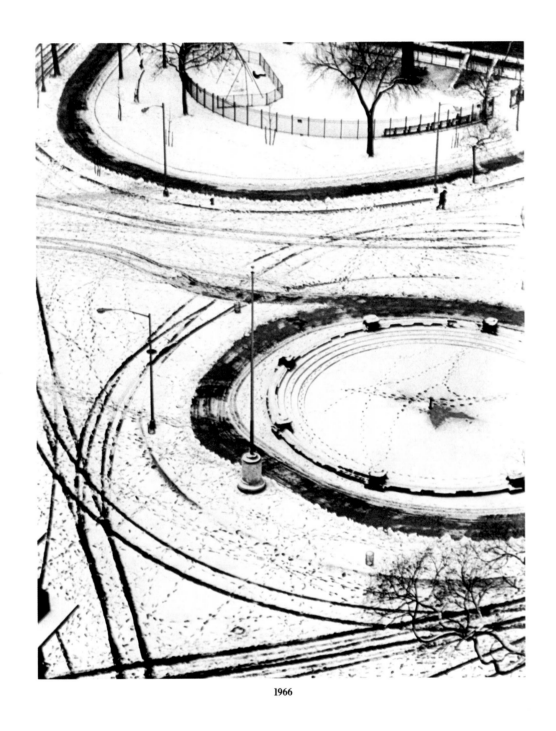

1966

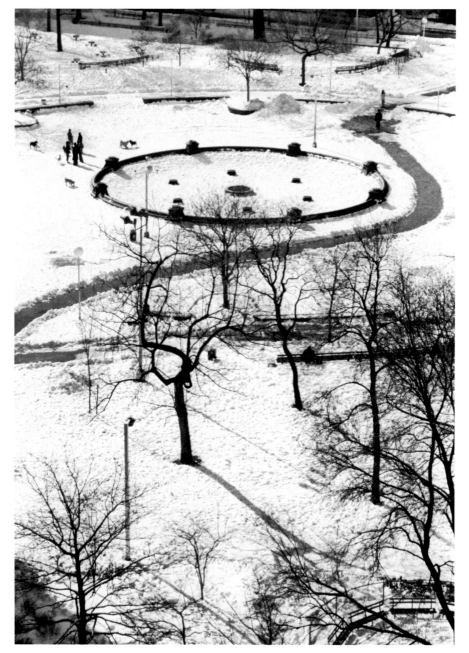

1978

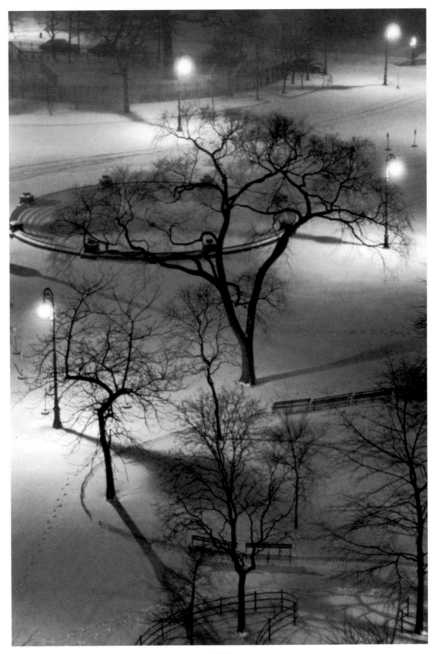

1954

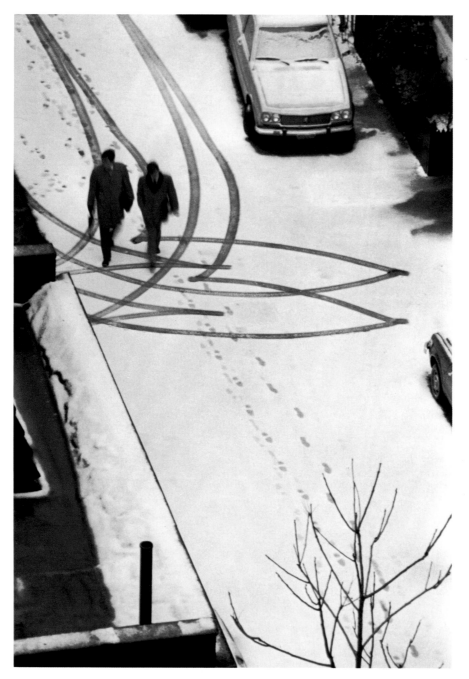

1977

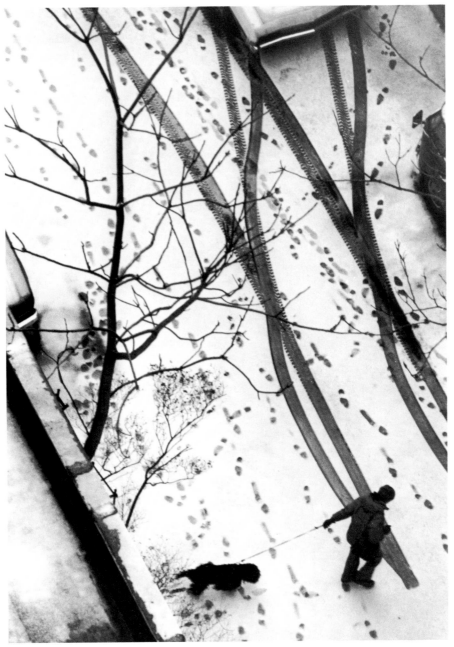

1977

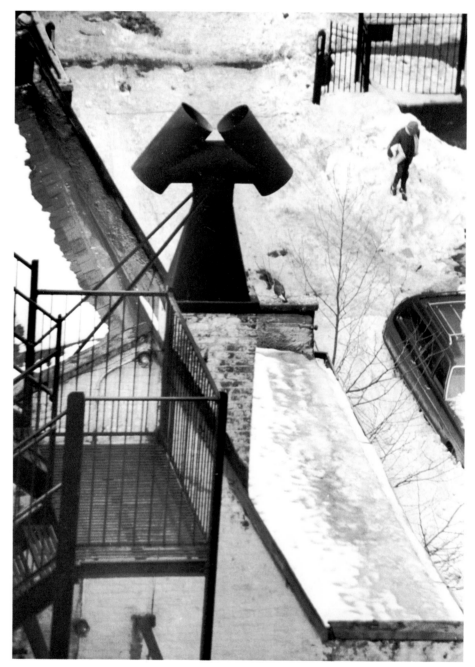

1978

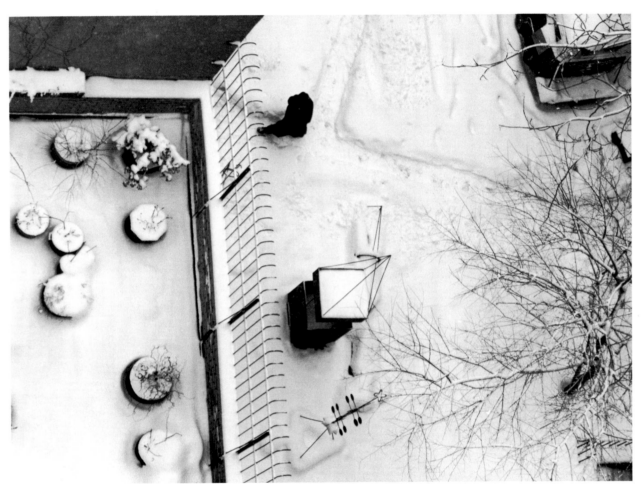

1978

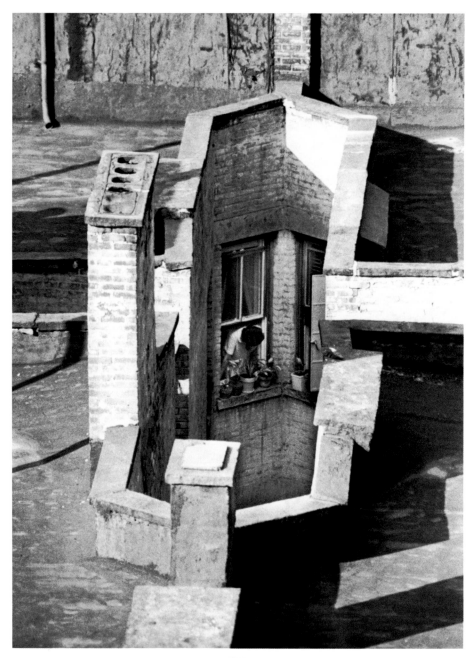

1970

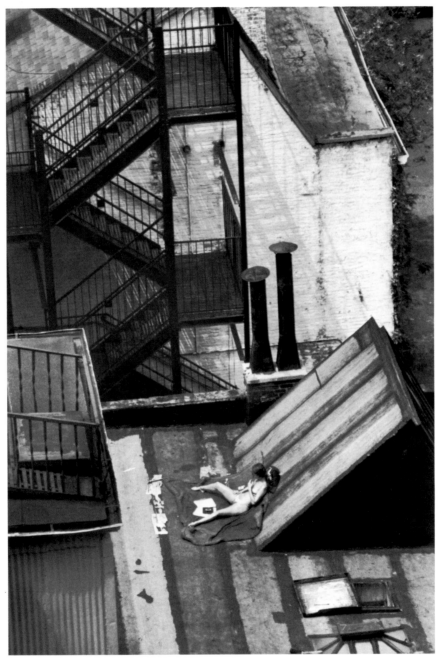

1978

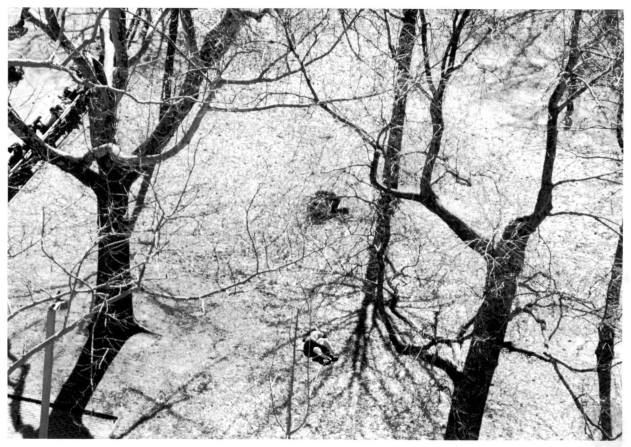

1978

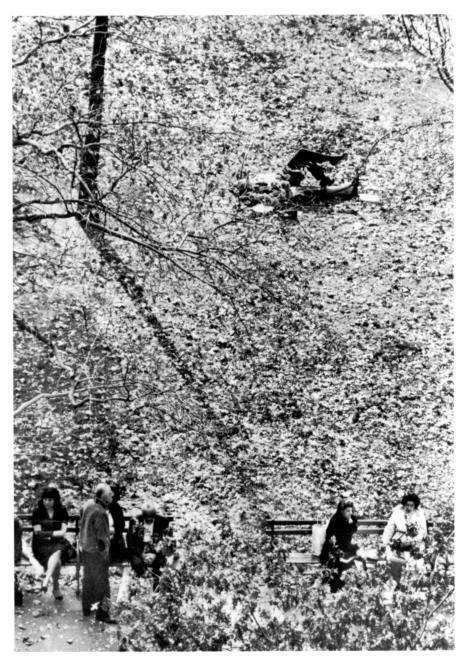

1964

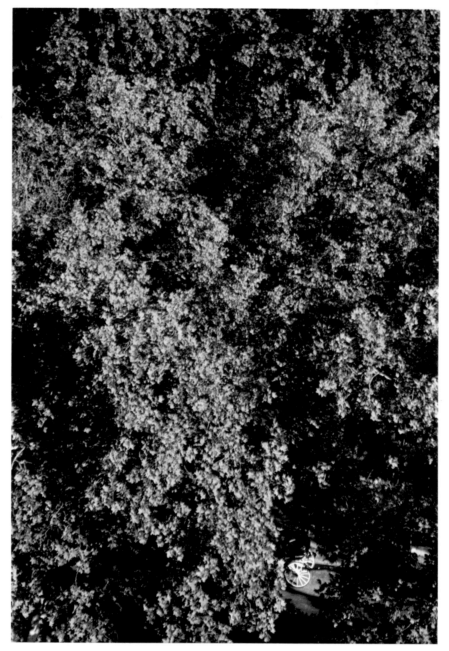

1975

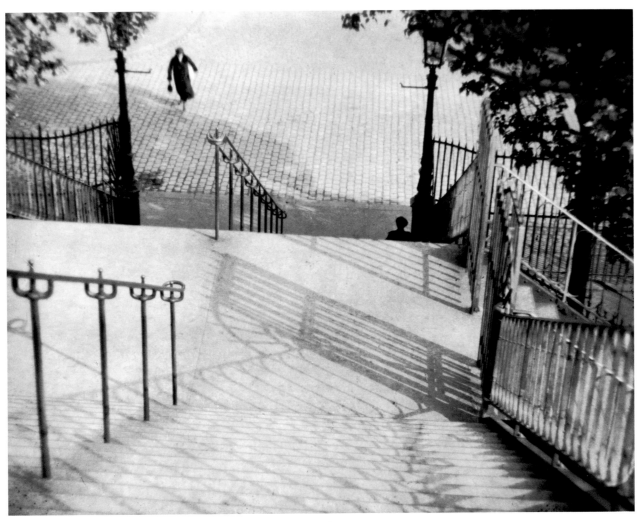

1925

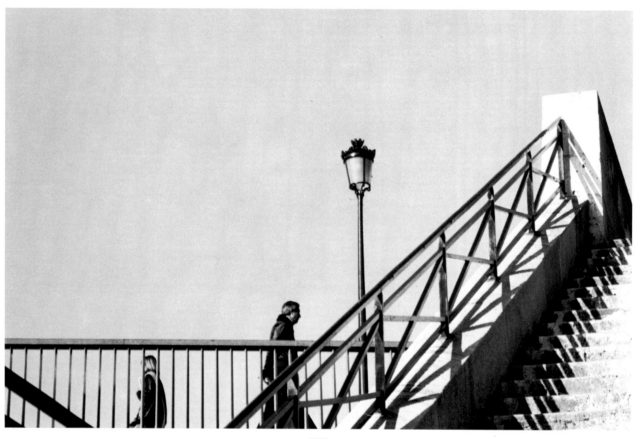

1980

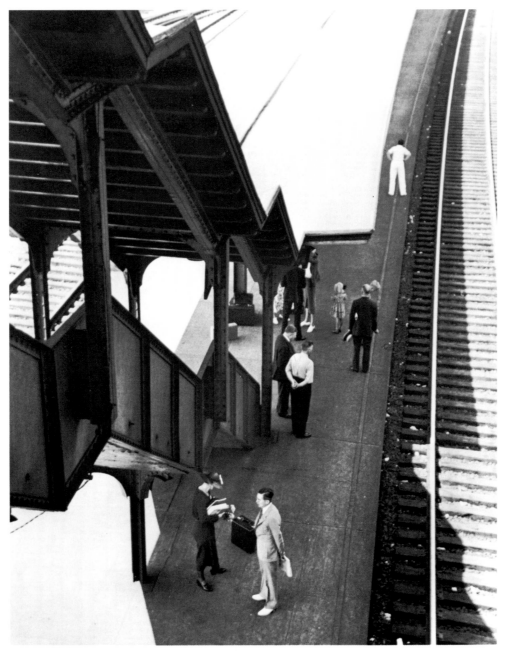

1937

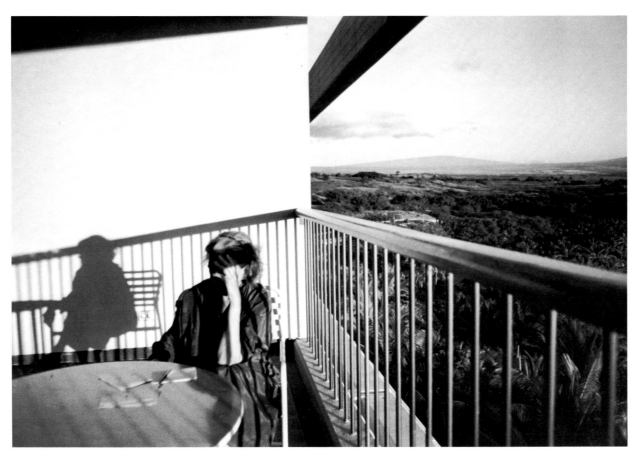

1974

1972

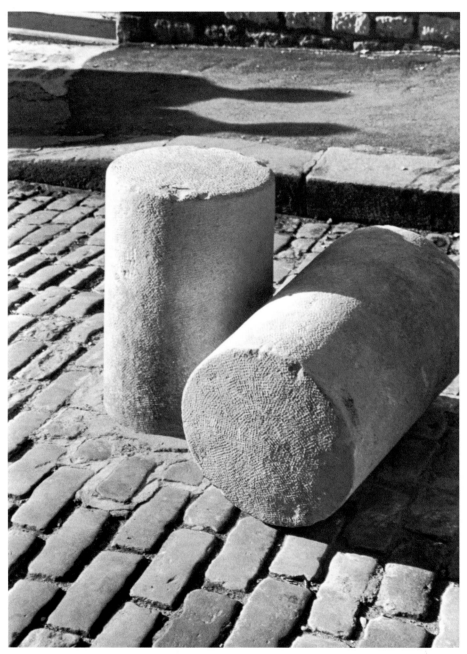

1980

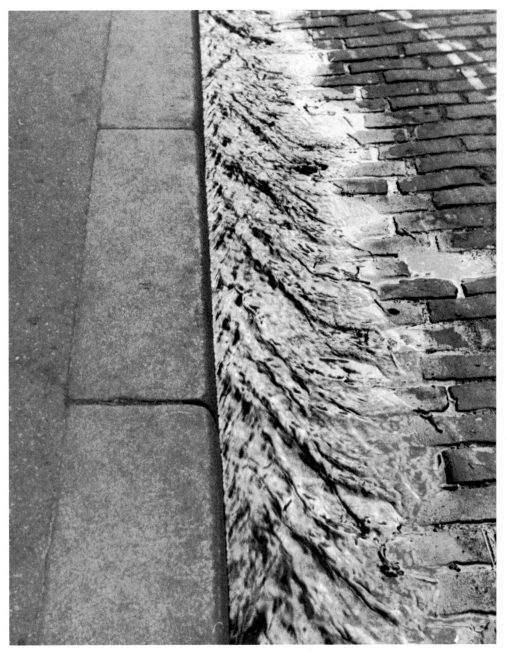

1929

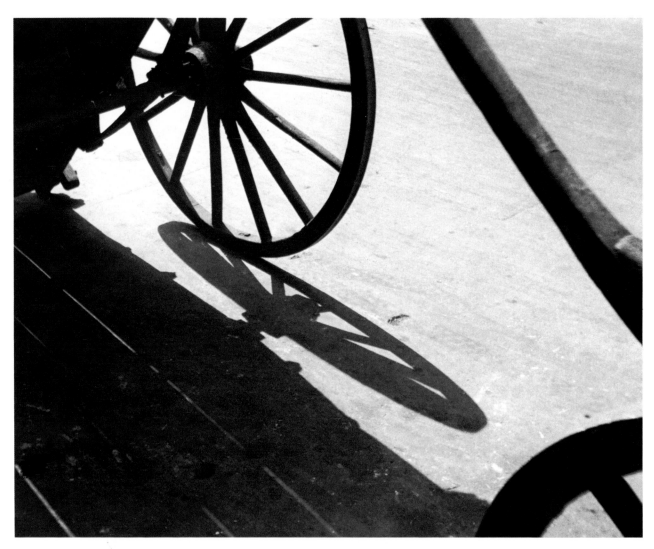

1928

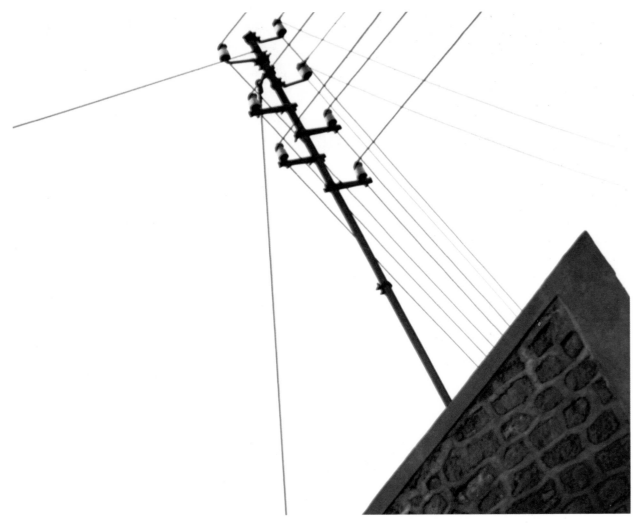

1927

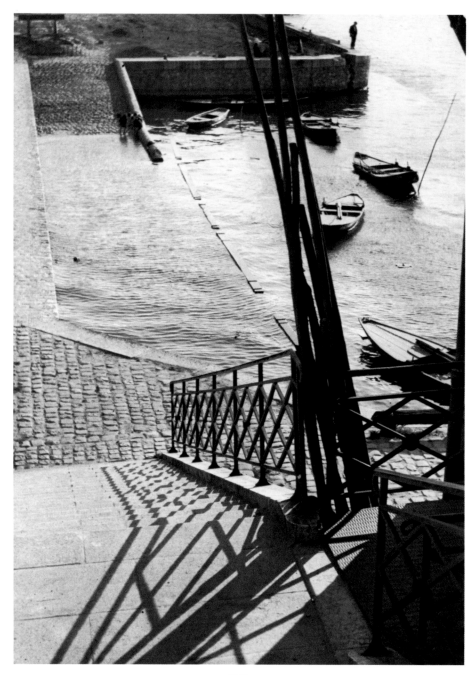

1927

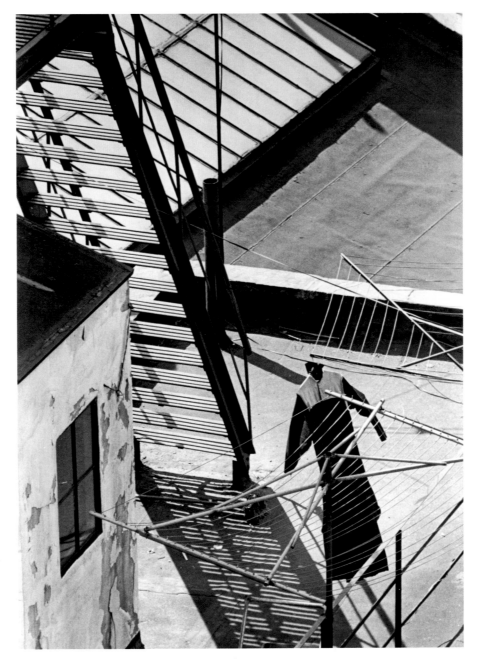

1963

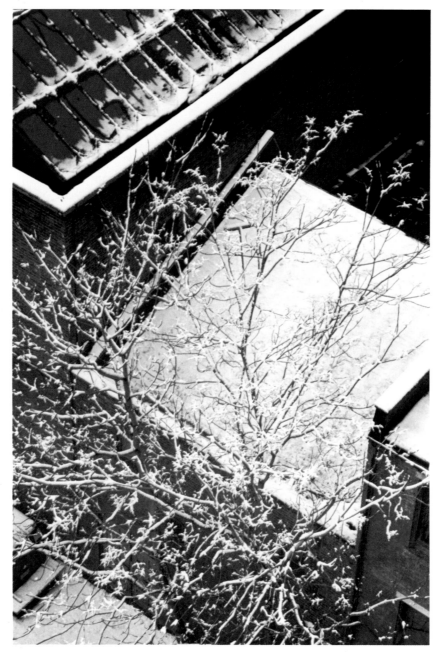

1977

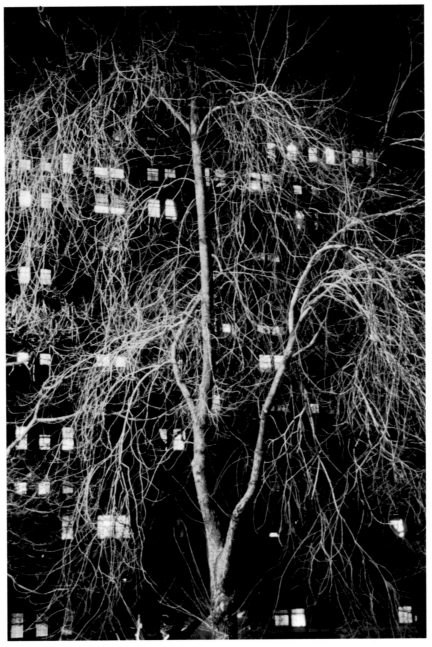

1958

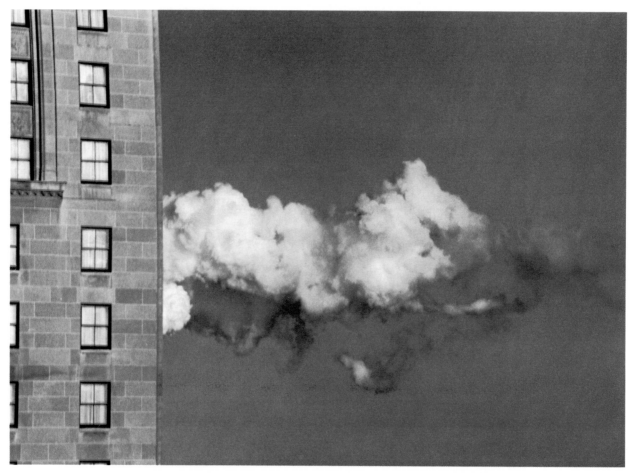

1979

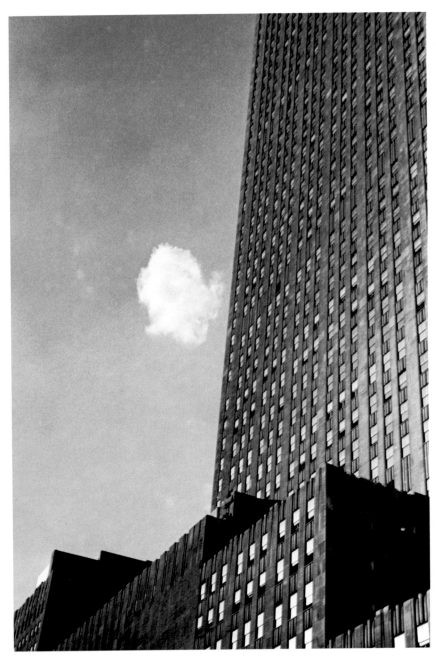

1937

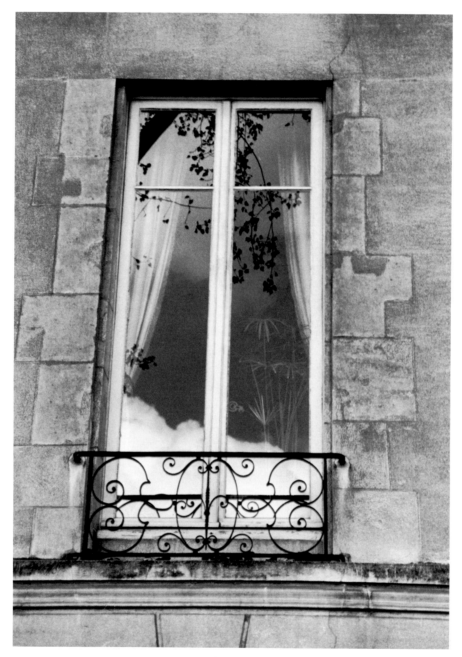

1980

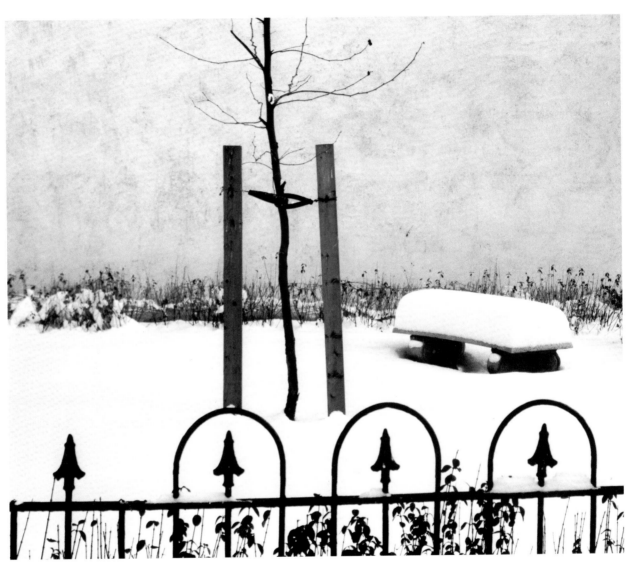

1959

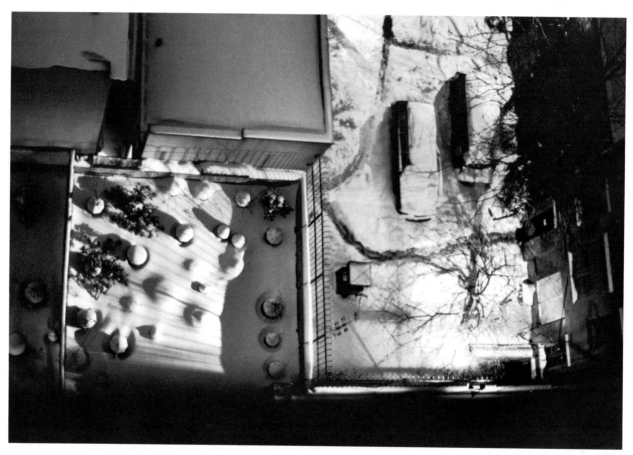

1978

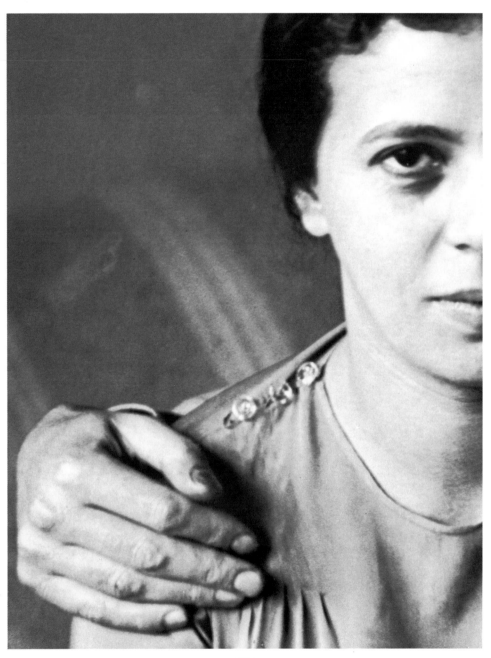

1931

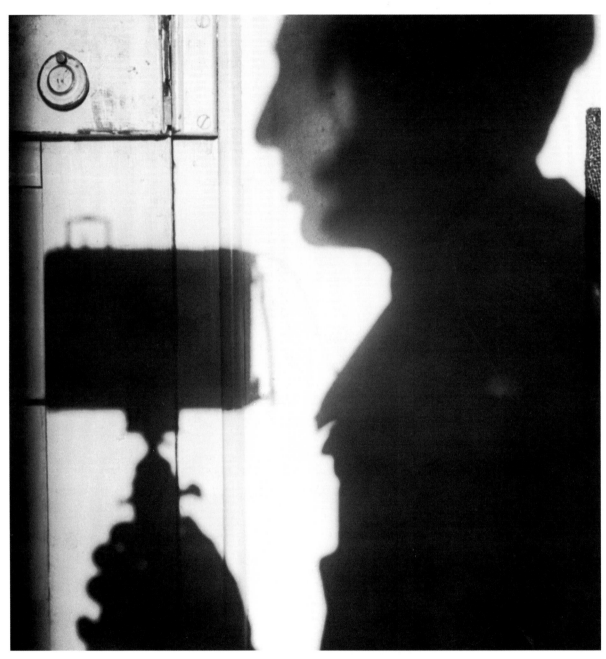

1927

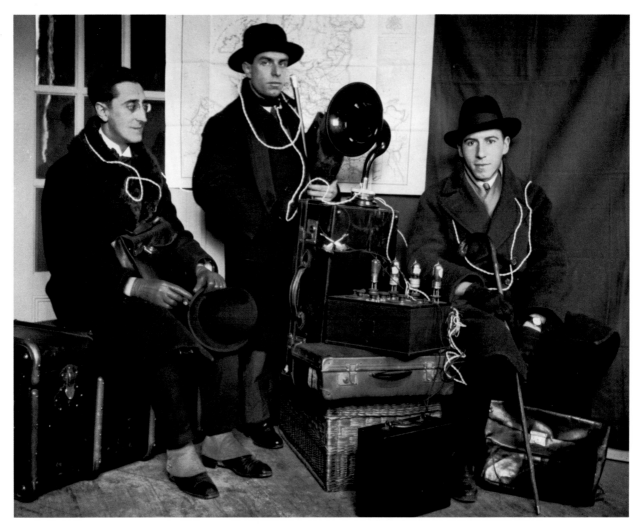

1927

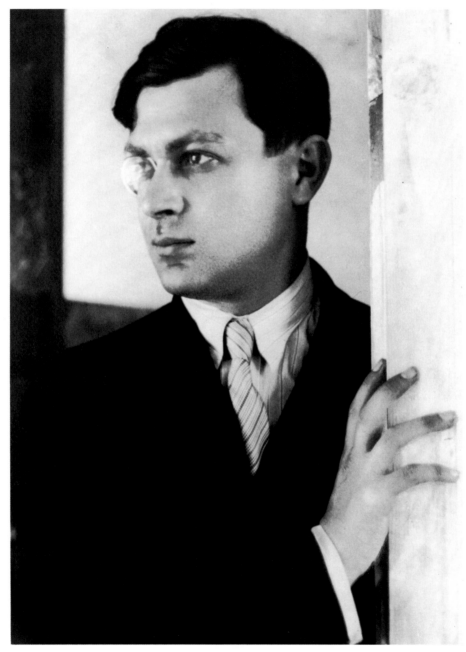

1926

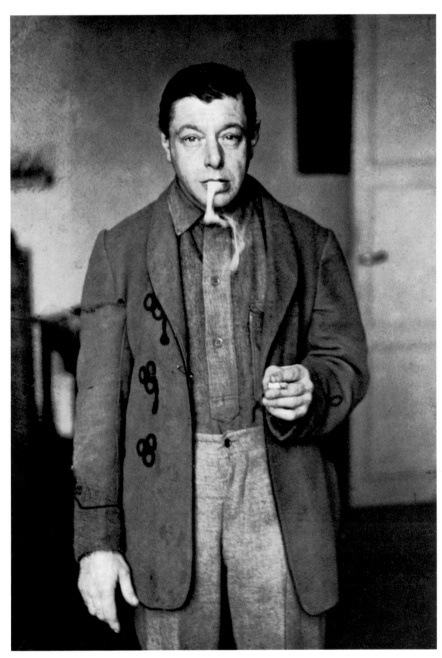

1926

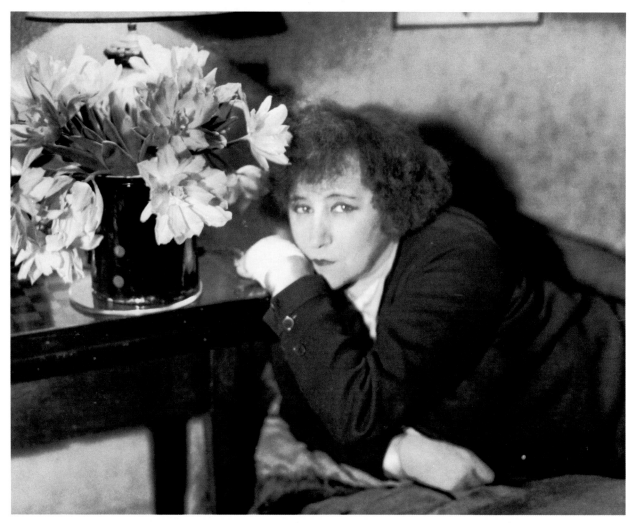

1930

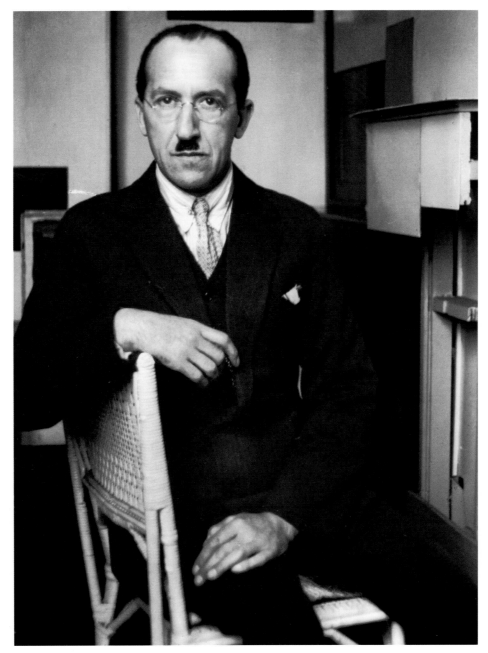

1926

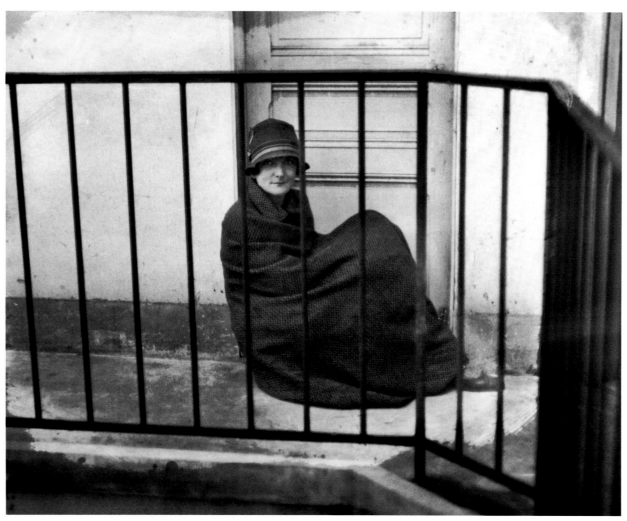

1927

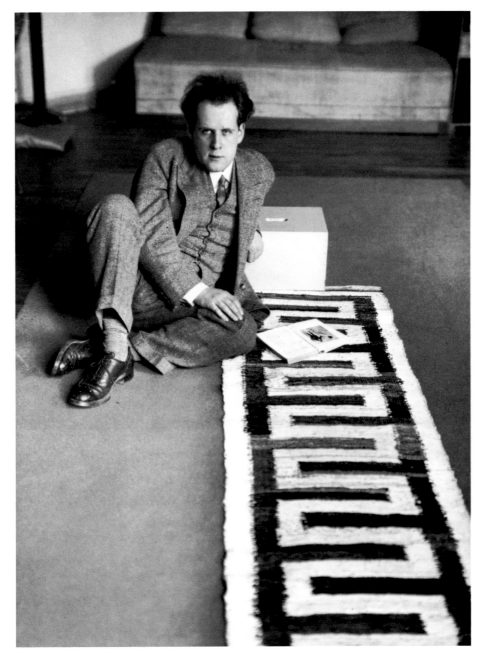

1929

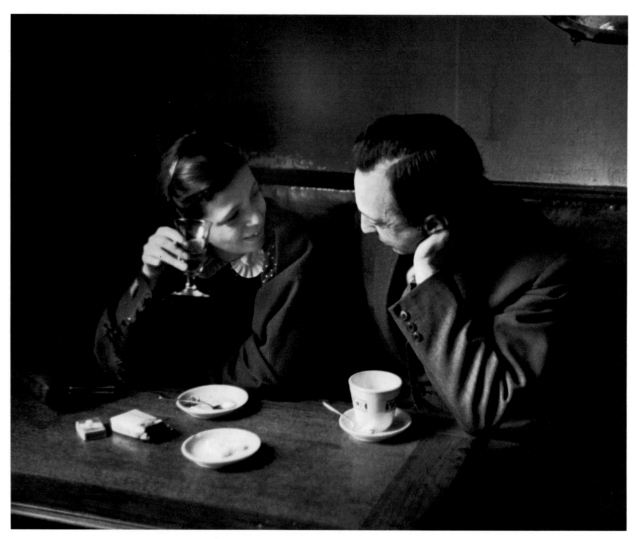

1931

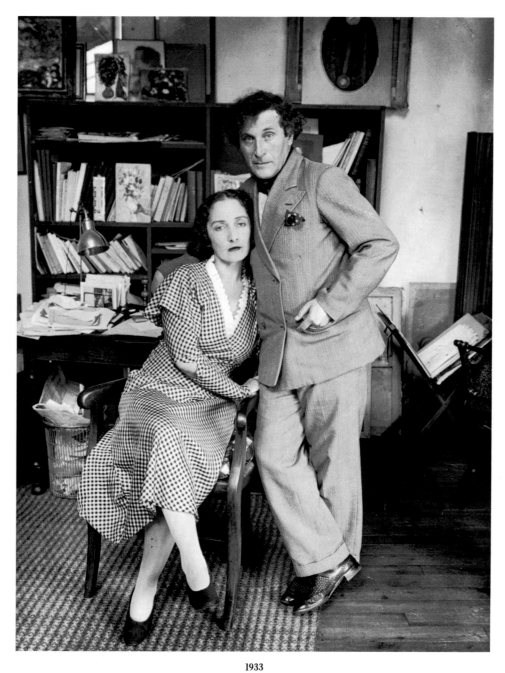

1933

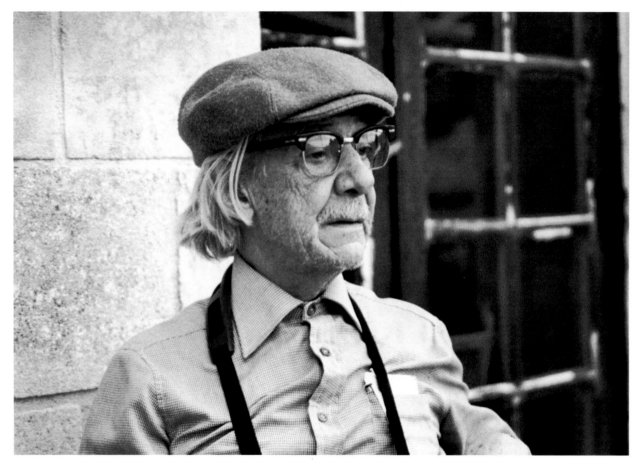

1979

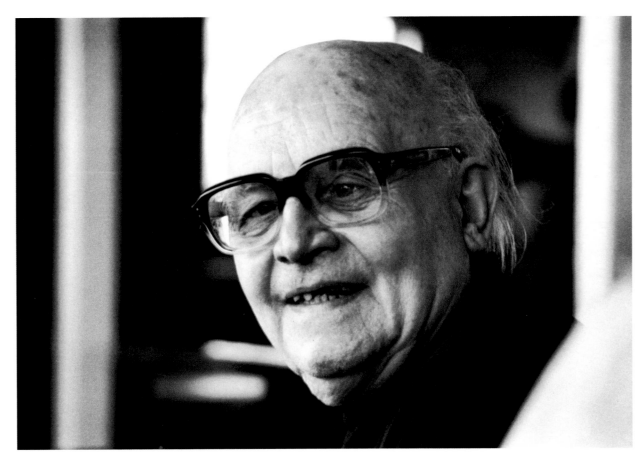

1979

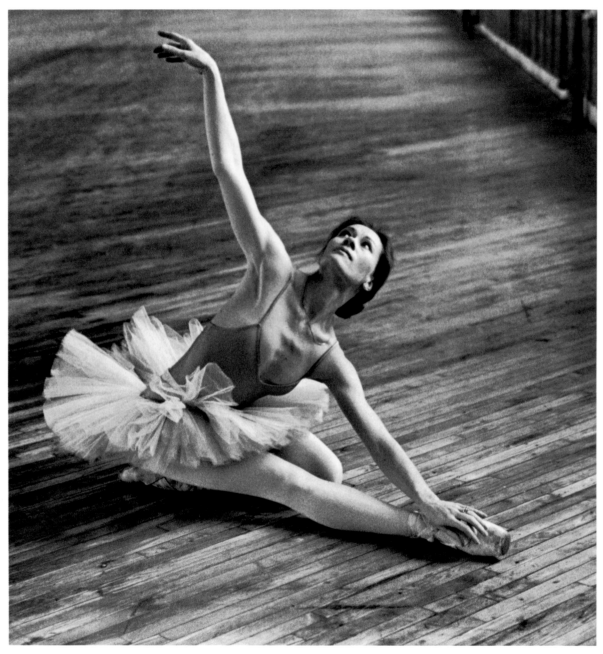

1981

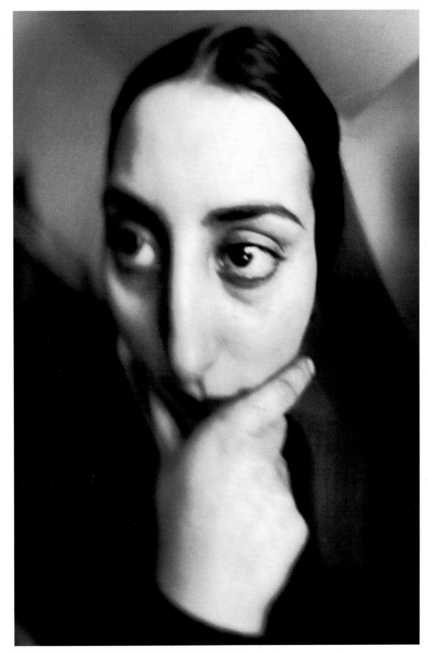

1927

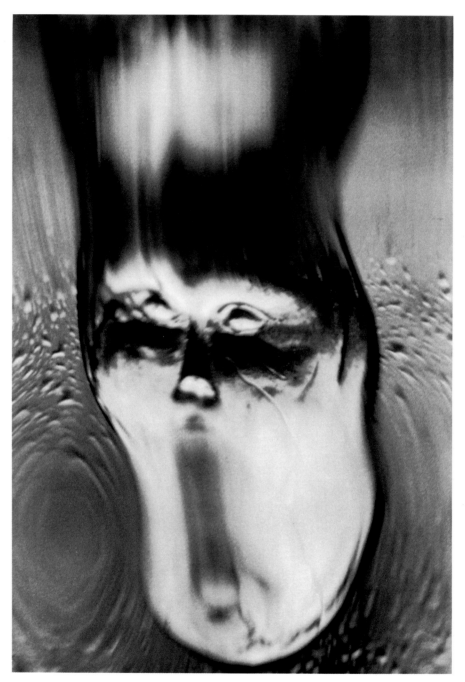

1967

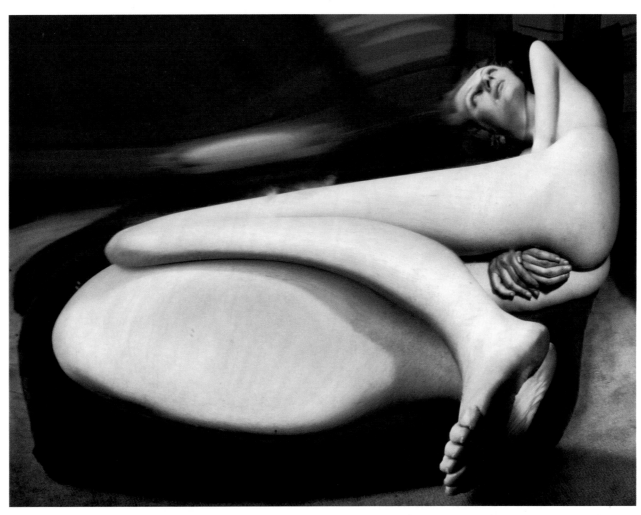

1933

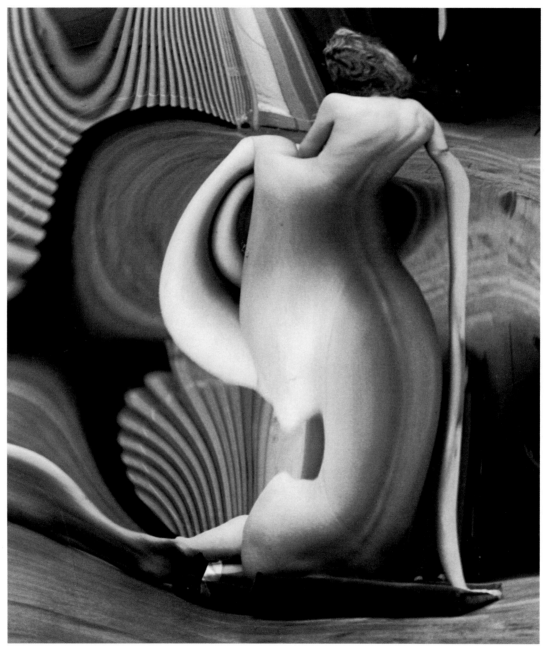

1933

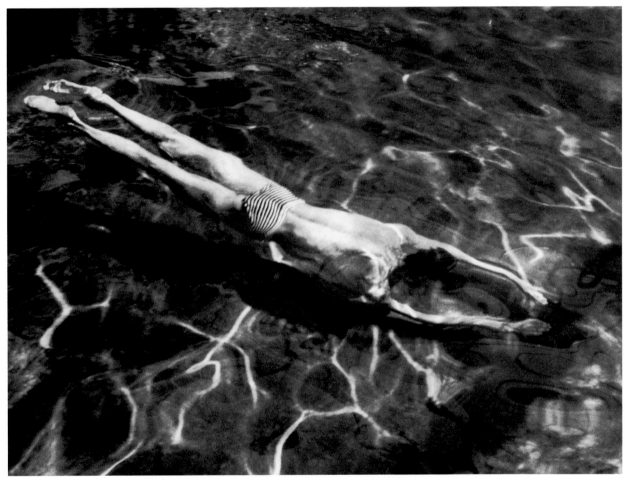

1917

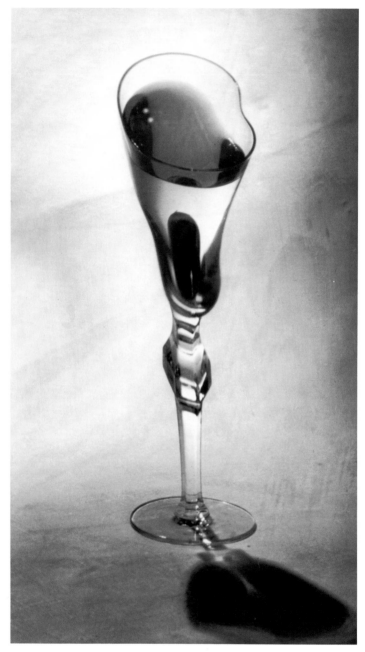

1943

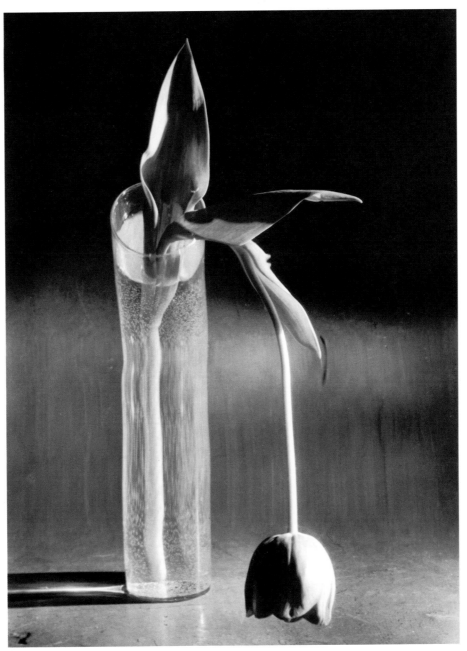

1939

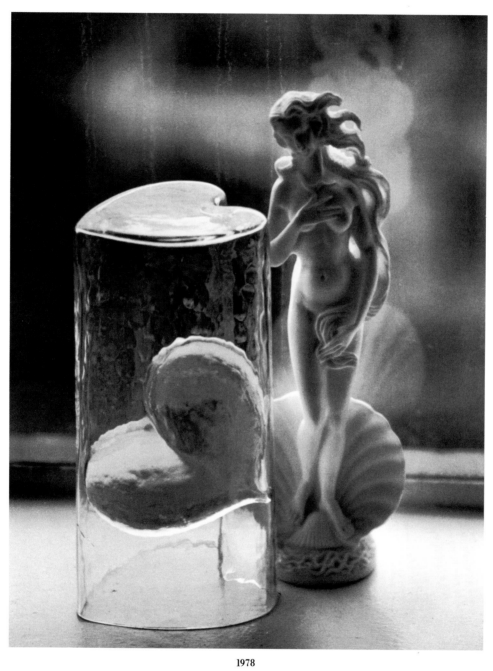

1978

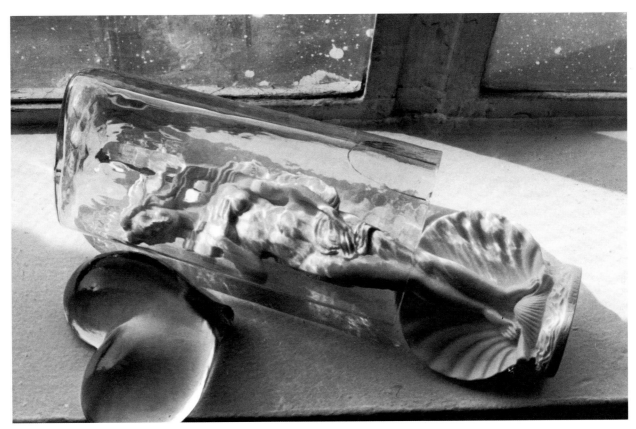

1978

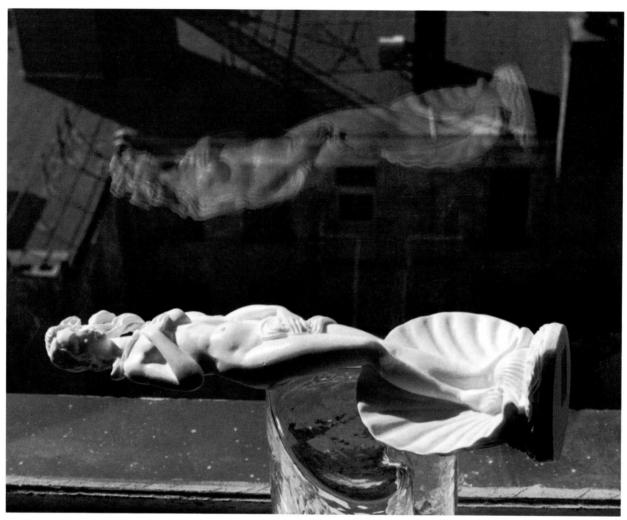

1978

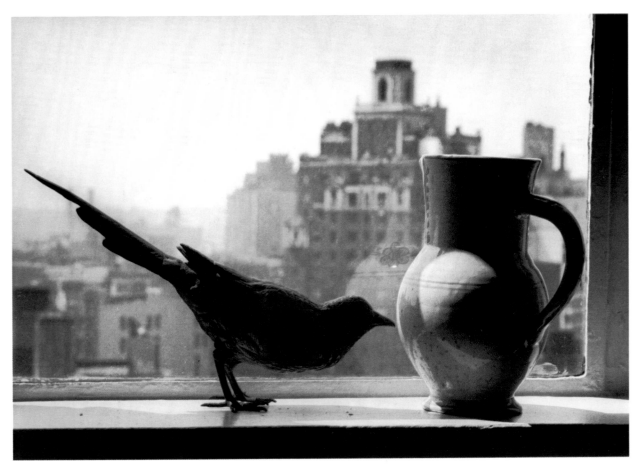

1976

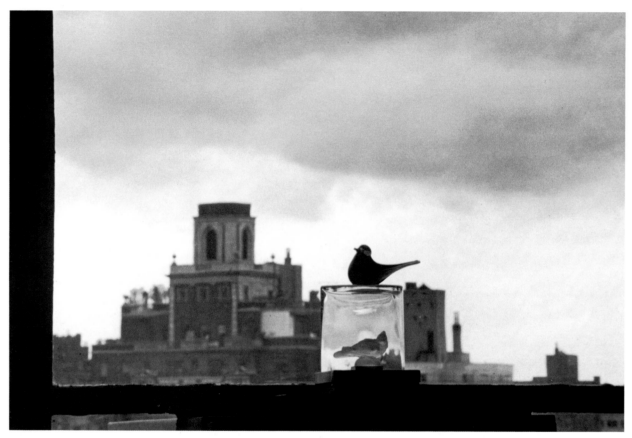

1978

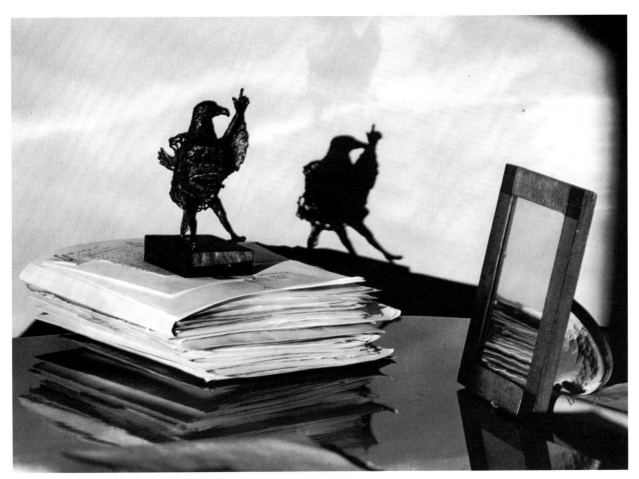

1978

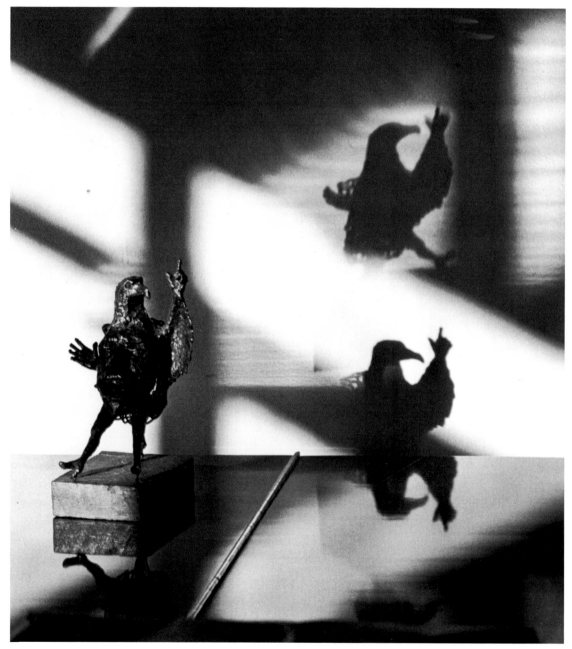

1978

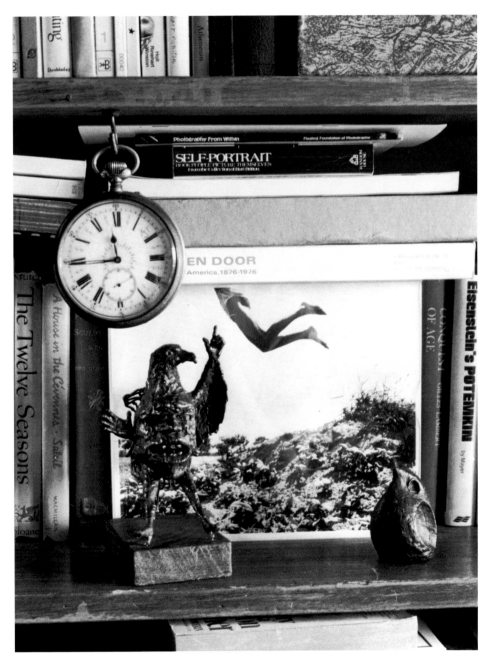

1978

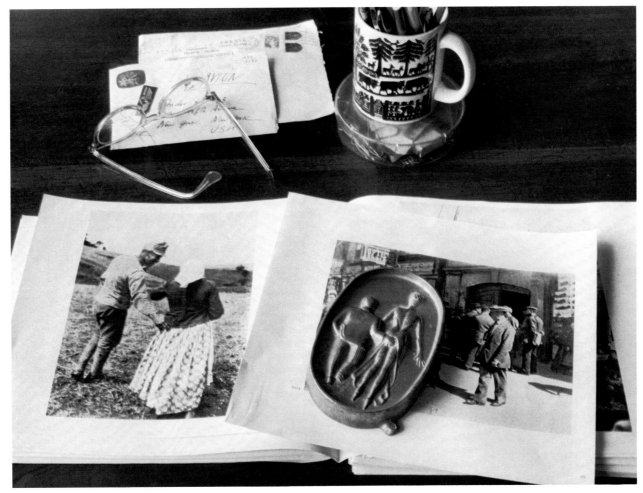

1978

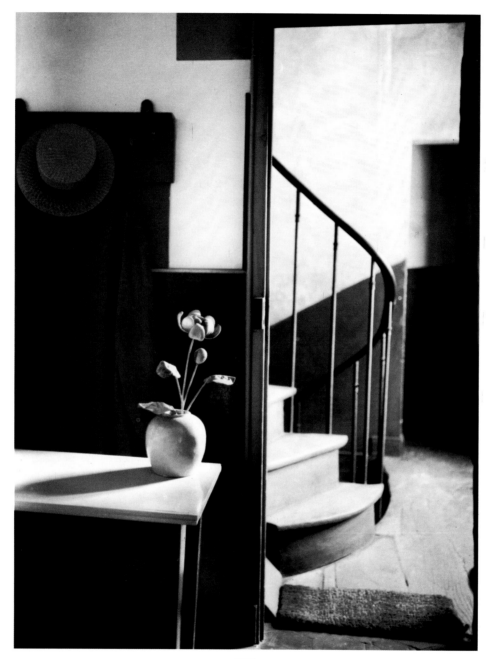

1926

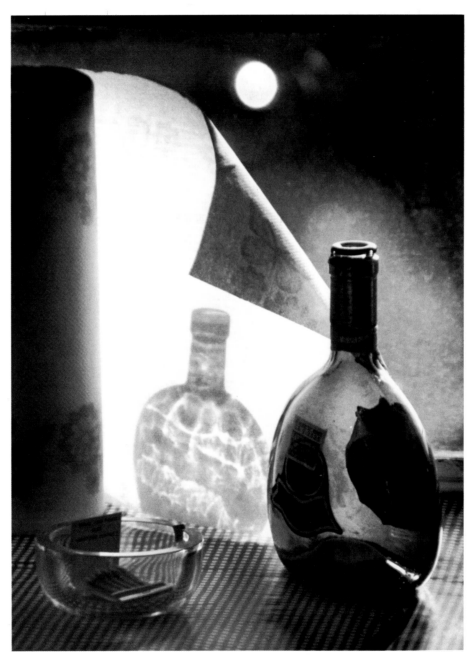

1974

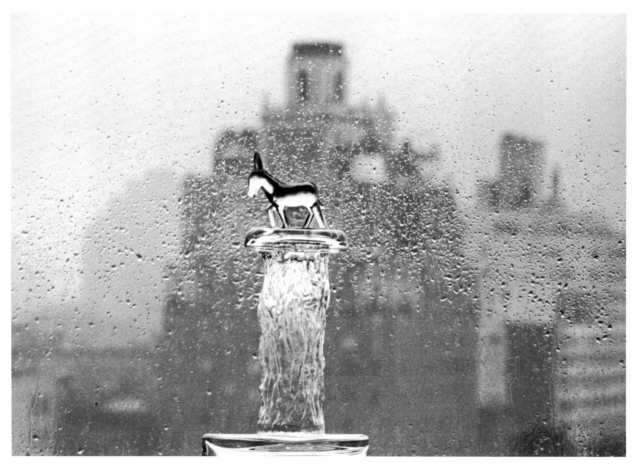

1977

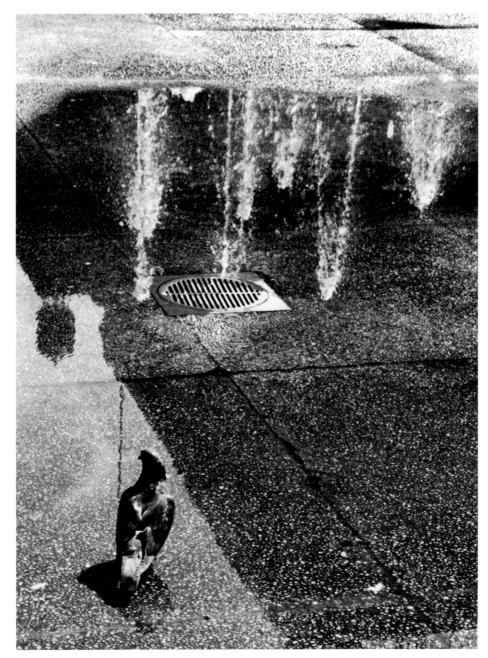

1978

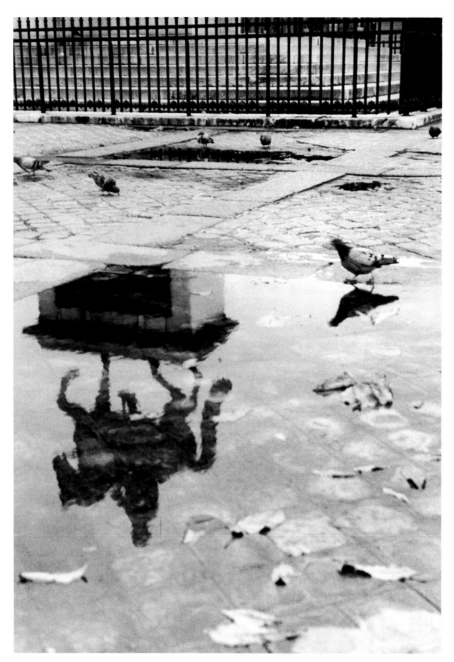

1963

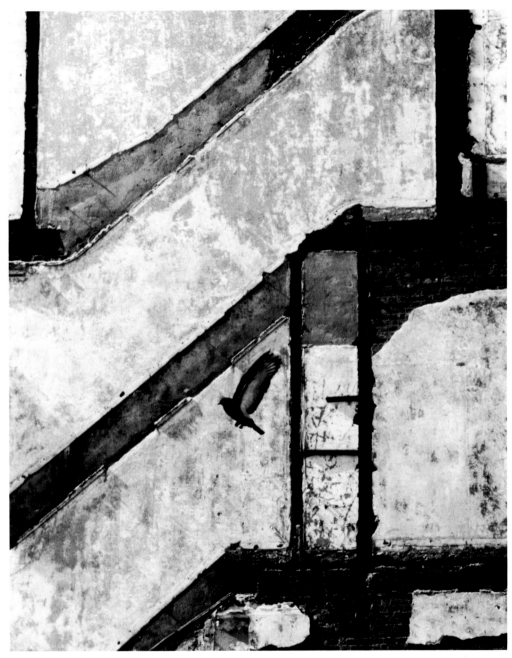

1960

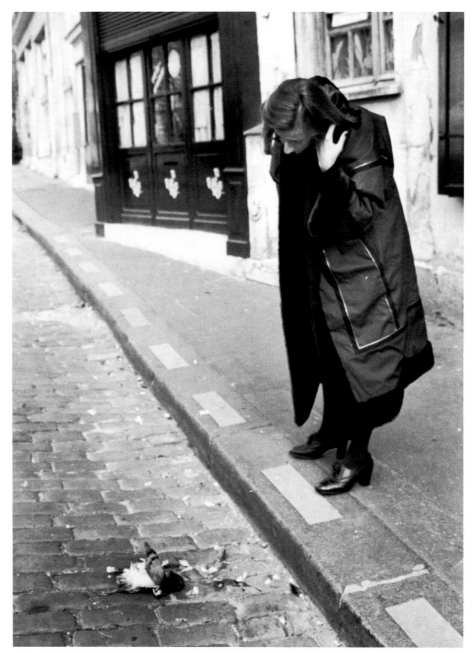

1980

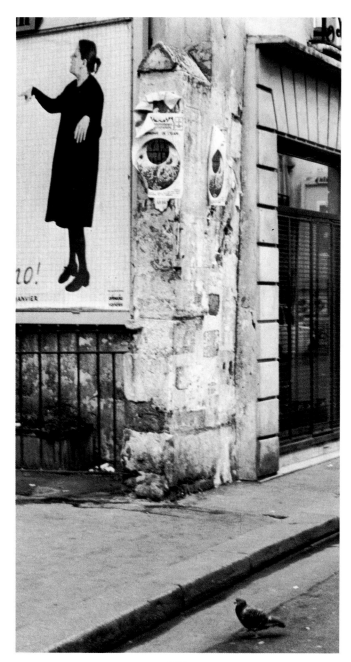

1980

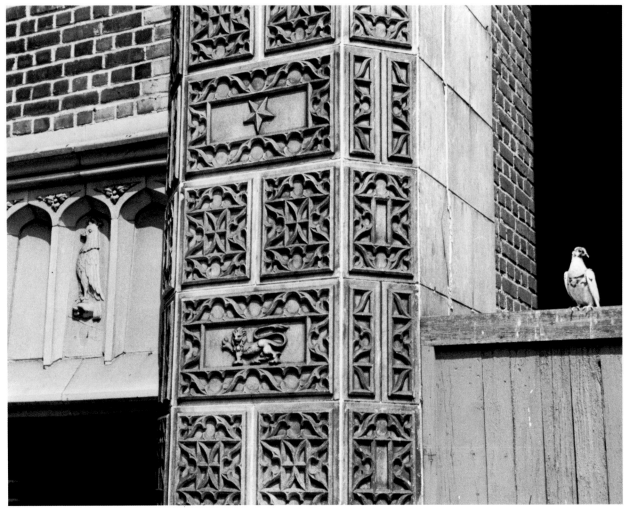

1962

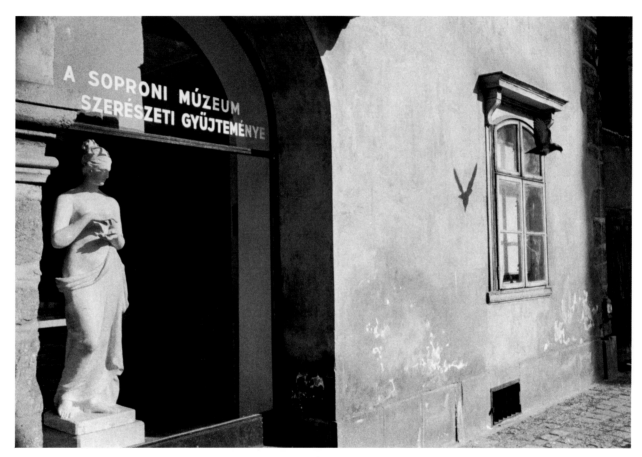

1971

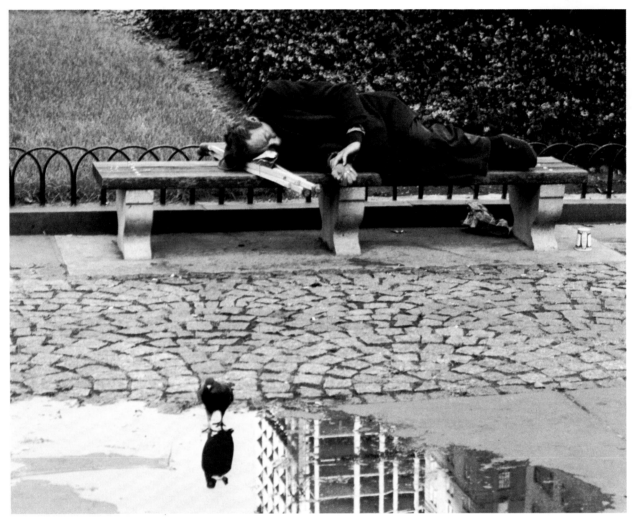

1977

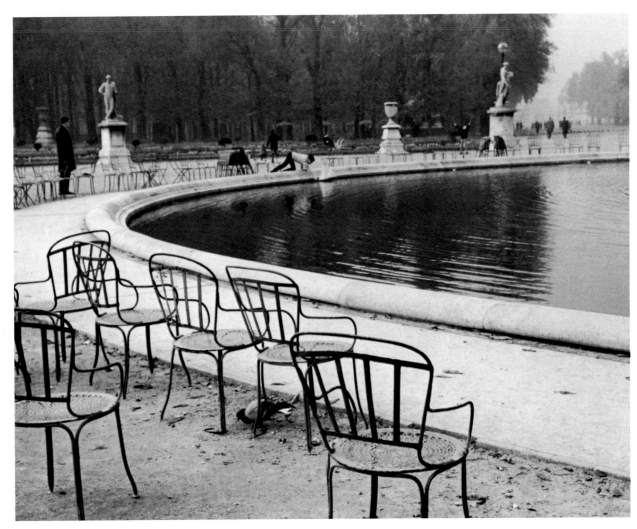

1963

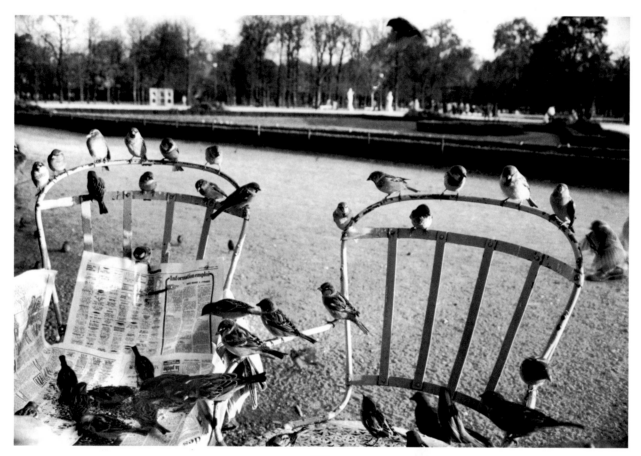

1980

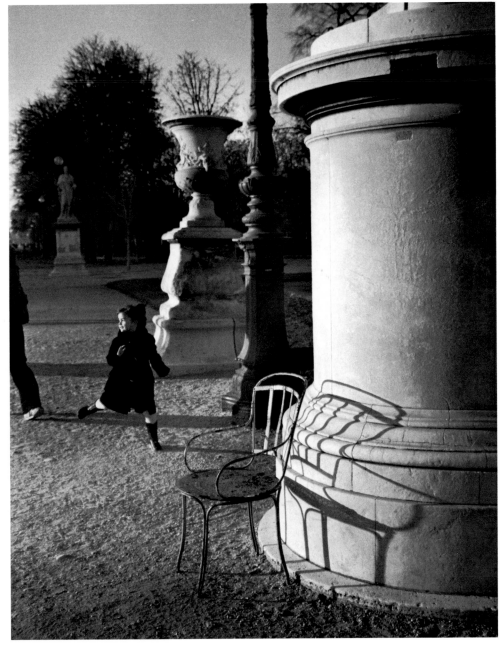

1980

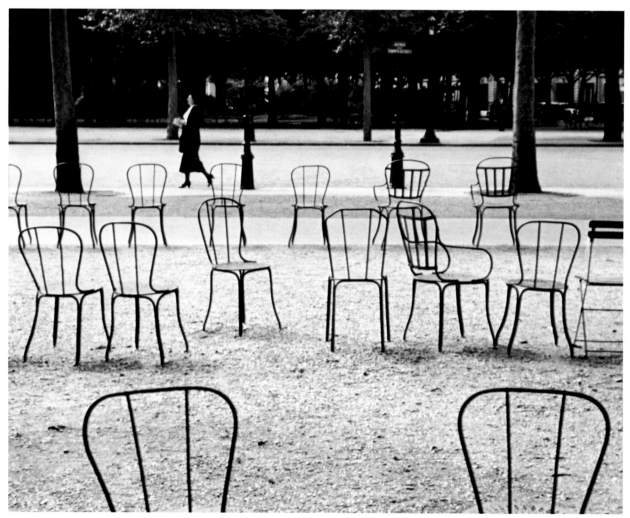

1927

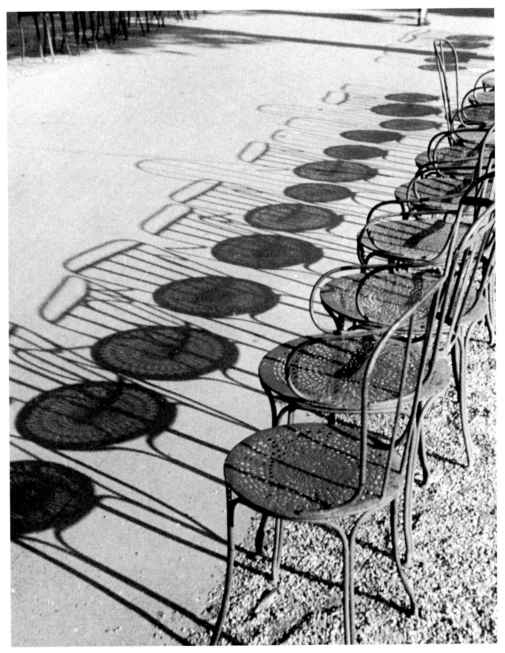

1929

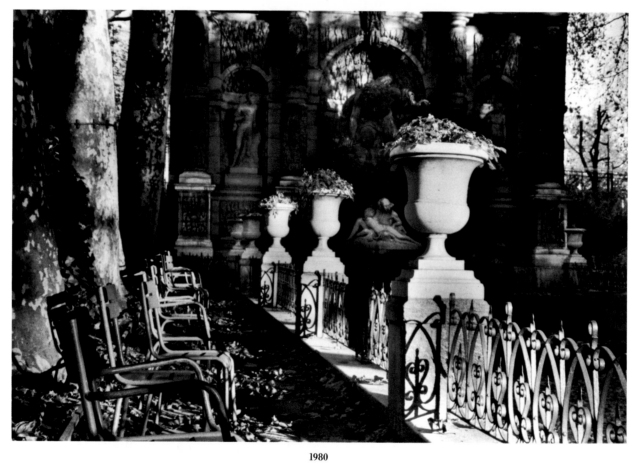

1980

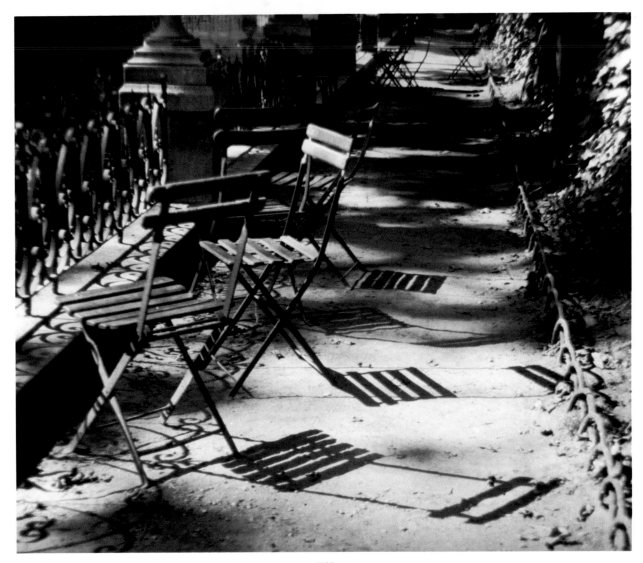

1925

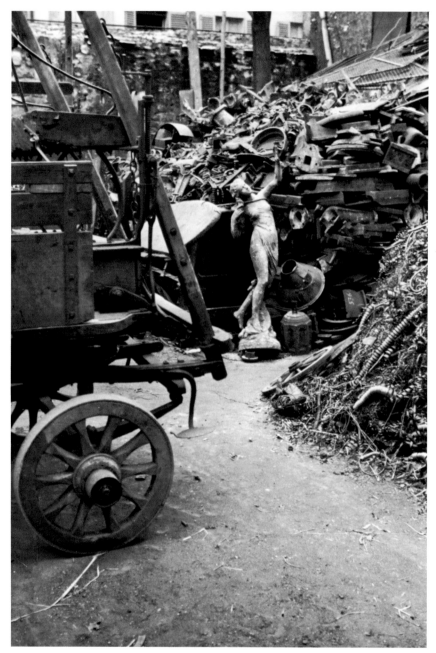

1930

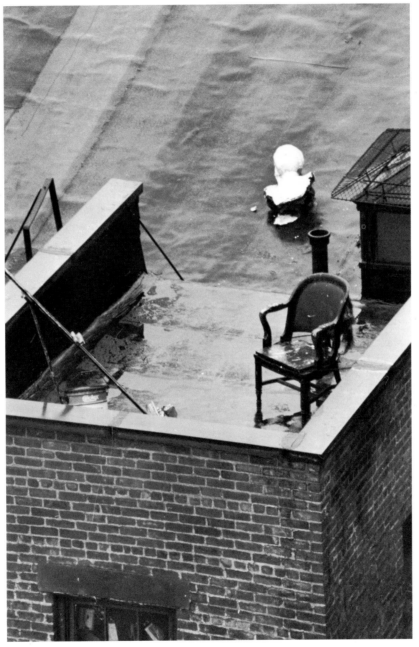

1977

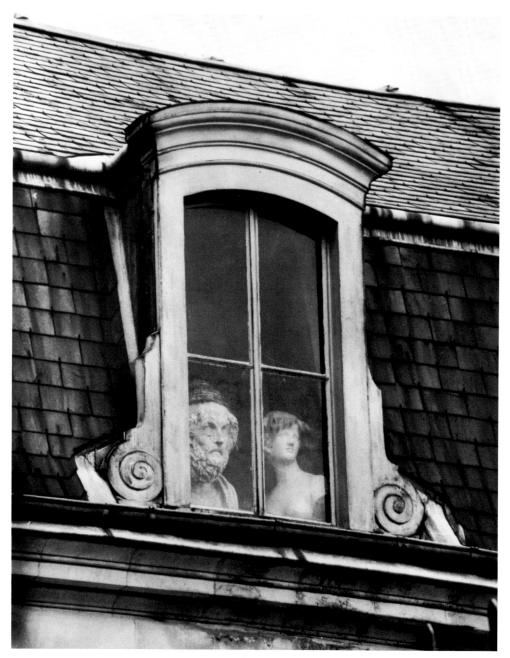

1928

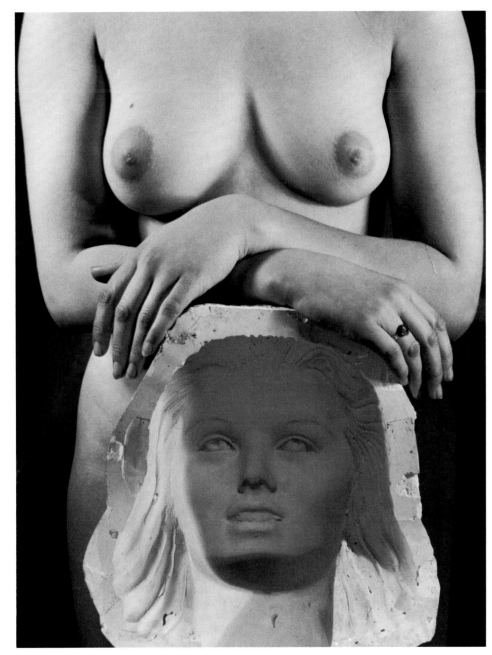

1939

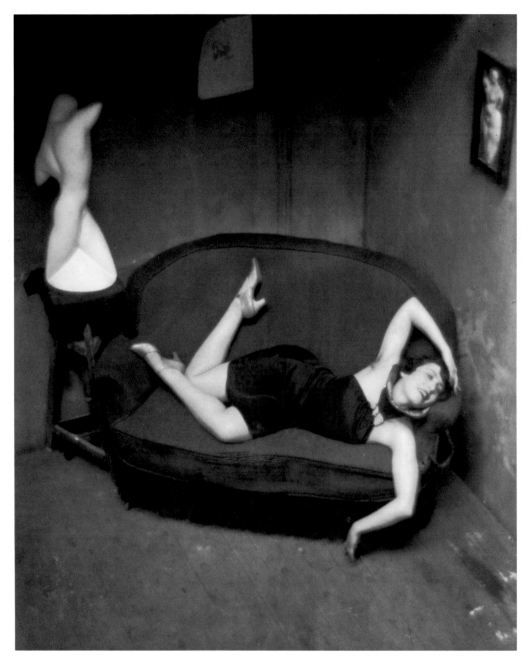

1926

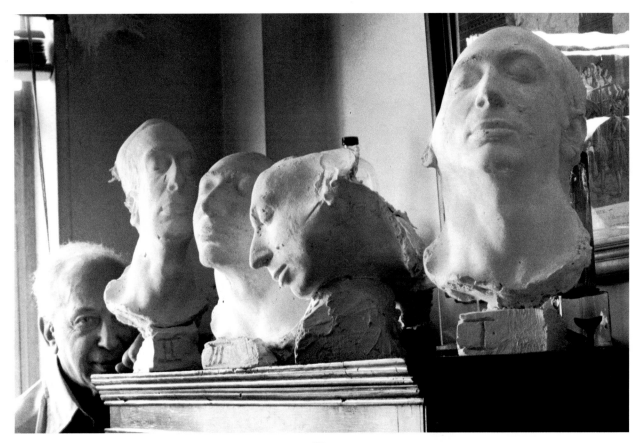

1976

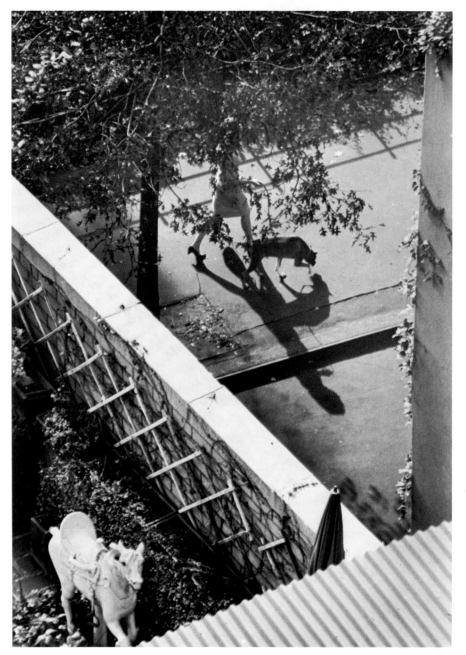

1962

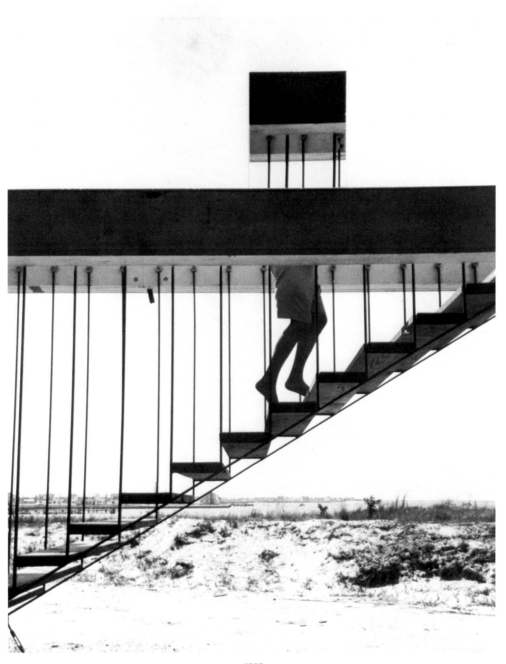

1955

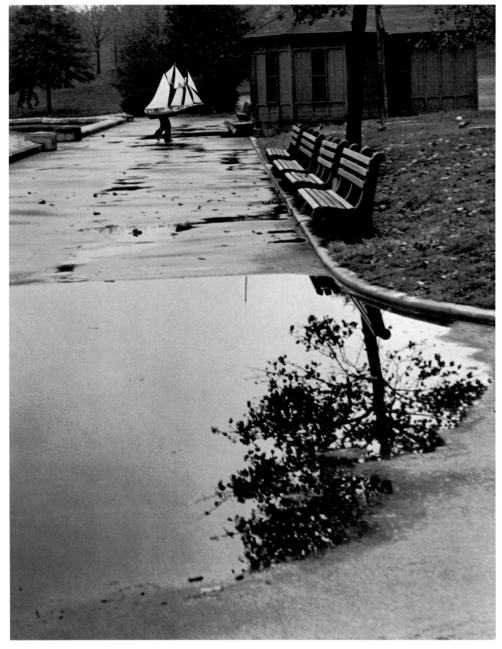

1944

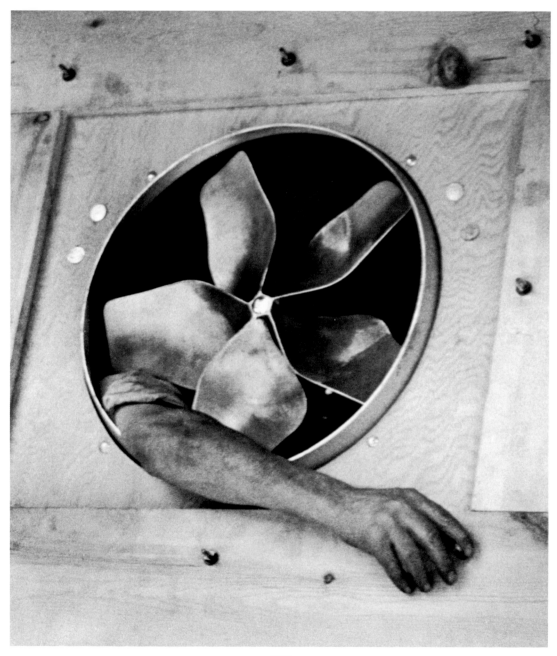

1937

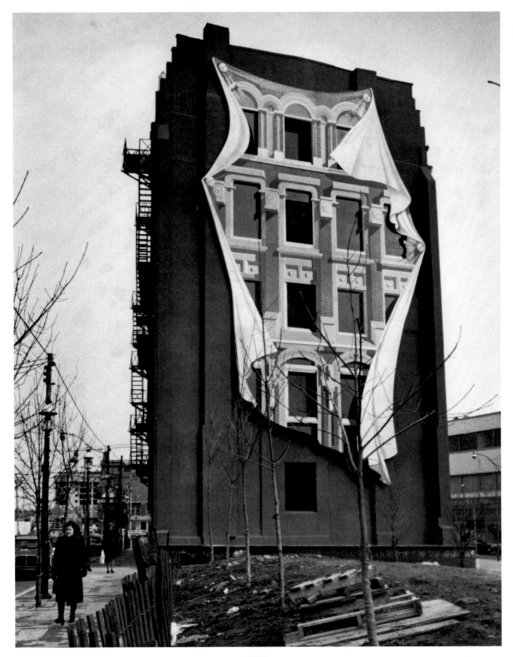

1981

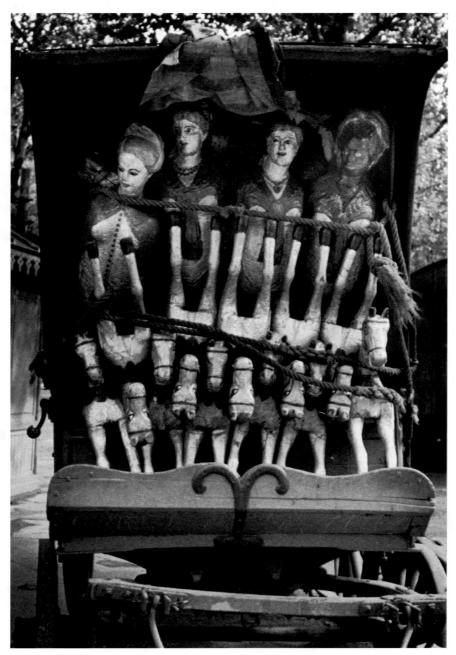

1929

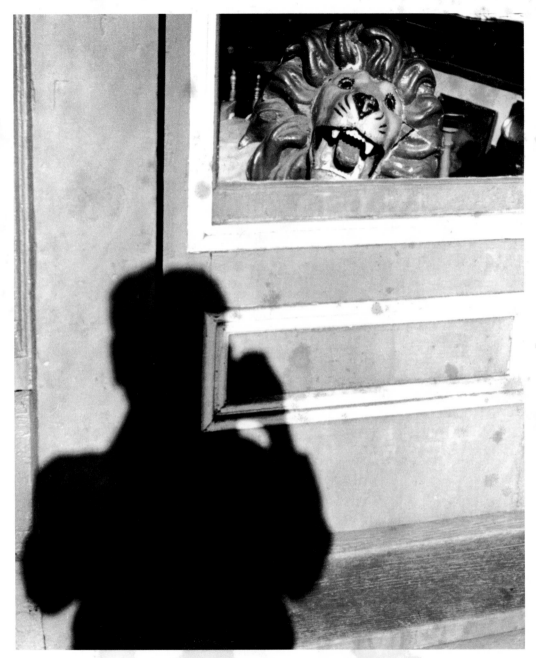

1942